HOME OFFICE

THE POLICE DRIVERS' MANUAL

LONDON: HMSO

ISBN 0 11 340721 1

INTRODUCTION

This booklet, which succeeds former versions of *Roadcraft*, has been prepared by police officers and embodies the knowledge and experience gained through years of driving under all conditions.

Accidents, with rare exceptions, do not occur at any given times and places, but rather in widely scattered areas and at all times of the day and night. Comparatively few of these incidents can be directly attributed to any particular road feature or vehicle defect, but it is found that in nine cases out of ten the cause of the accident can be traced to the failure of the 'human element' of the person or persons concerned.

The aim of the following chapters is to raise the reader's standard of driving to the highest possible degree of all-round efficiency. A vehicle can be a lethal weapon and, like a gun, it should be handled with care; the advice which follows is not intended to reduce the pleasure to be gained from driving, in fact the opposite is true, the more confidence and knowledge at a driver's disposal, the greater is his capacity for enjoying and taking pride in his driving. Furthermore, if the reader follows this advice he may one day save somebody's life — perhaps his own.

CONTENTS

CONTENTS

CONTENTS

CHAPTER 1

THE SYSTEM OF CAR CONTROL

Introduction

1 The prevention of road accidents has been a matter for public concern ever since vehicles first appeared. Accidents can occur at any time and place and cannot be attributed to any particular road feature or vehicle defect.

2 A common factor in accidents in which a vehicle is involved is the presence of a human being and the probability of human error. The human element is directly responsible for almost every accident and it is upon this aspect that attention must be focussed. In addition to a high degree of skill, drivers must show restraint and courtesy and the spirit of tolerance and consideration for others underlying the provisions of the Highway Code.

3 Many schemes and regulations have been introduced from time to time to try and reduce the number of accidents, but the most consistently successful has been the continued presence of the Police motor patrols, who supervise the behaviour of other road users. Their own standard of driving must therefore be above reproach if they are to set a proper example and gain the respect and co-operation essential to their task.

4 The object of this manual is to raise the level of driving by teaching a uniform and methodical system which will provide an increased margin of safety at all times.

5 Driving includes starting a vehicle, moving off, accelerating, steering it over different road surfaces, round bends and corners, in and out of premises, past other vehicles, progressing steadily through traffic, travelling at high speed if necessary, slowing down and eventually, stopping. All this has to be done in complete safety, with no inconvenience to others and with minimum wear to the vehicle.

6 Quiet efficiency is the hallmark of the expert. Although alert he gives the impression of being completely relaxed. He drives in a calm, controlled style without fuss or flourish, progressing smoothly and unobtrusively. He will always be in the right place on the road, travelling at the right speed with the right gear engaged and he achieves this desirable state by concentrating all the time, planning ahead and driving systematically.

7 The driver of a vehicle has a great deal to think about as continually changing conditions demand frequent alterations in course and speed. The surrounding traffic situation must be taken into account, including the proximity of other vehicles, the need to signal intentions, the surface conditions; in fact, a host of items to be thought about all the time.

8 The Police System of Car Control creates a simple and repetitive method of driving which ensures that the driver omits no detail, leaves nothing to chance and when perfected gives that one ingredient essential to safe driving—TIME TO REACT.

Definitions

9 THE SYSTEM OF CAR CONTROL IS A SYSTEM OR DRILL, EACH FEATURE OF WHICH IS CONSIDERED, IN SEQUENCE, BY THE DRIVER AT THE APPROACH TO ANY HAZARD. It is the basis upon which the whole technique of good driving is built.

10 A hazard is anything which contains an element of actual or potential danger.

There are three main types:

    (a) physical features, such as a junction, roundabout, bend or hill crest;

    (b) those created by the position or movement of other road users; and

    (c) those created by variations in road surface or weather conditions.

11 By definition every feature of the System is considered at the approach to any hazard. Only those applicable to the particular circumstances are put into operation but whichever features are selected they must always be in the correct sequence. It is only by constant practice that skill in the application of the System can be acquired.

Features of the System

12 The FEATURES of the System of Car Control are as follows:

    (1) COURSE—The driver, having seen the hazard, decides on the correct line of approach. He looks in his mirrors and if it is necessary to change position to obtain the correct course, he considers a deviation signal.

    (2) MIRRORS, SIGNALS AND SPEED—The mirrors are again used and if the intention is to turn right or left at the hazard, consideration must be given to a deviation signal.

Any reduction in speed for the hazard will be accomplished at this stage preceded by a slowing down signal if appropriate.

(3) GEAR—The correct gear is selected for the speed of the vehicle following application of the second feature.

(4) MIRRORS AND SIGNALS—It is essential to look in the mirrors again and to consider a signal to deviate, if not previously given, or to emphasise an existing deviation signal.

(5) HORN—Sound the horn, if necessary.

(6) ACCELERATION—The correct degree of acceleration is applied to leave the hazard safely.

Application of the System
13 For all hazards the six features of the System of Car Control must be considered but any change in conditions on the approach may require a complete re-assessment, starting again at Feature One. For the purpose of the following examples it is assumed that the appropriate features can be applied without anything arising which might call for a change of plan.

RIGHT TURN
14 One of the most difficult and potentially dangerous manoeuvres is a right turn at cross roads because other road users may be entering the junction from any direction. The application of the System is illustrated in figure 1. As with all hazards the six features of the System of Car Control must be considered at the approach.

Feature One—Course
15 The ideal course is just left of the centre of the road or into a lane designated for right turn traffic. If travelling in the nearside it will be necessary to move out and this should be done in plenty of time having regard to the volume of traffic and the speed of approach to the hazard. Advanced information can be obtained from direction or warning signs relating to the junction. The mirrors must be used and a deviation signal given, if required, before moving out.

Feature Two—Mirrors, Signals and Speed
16 With the vehicle in the correct position on the road it will normally be necessary for the driver to reduce speed to that required to negotiate the turn safely. He must look in the

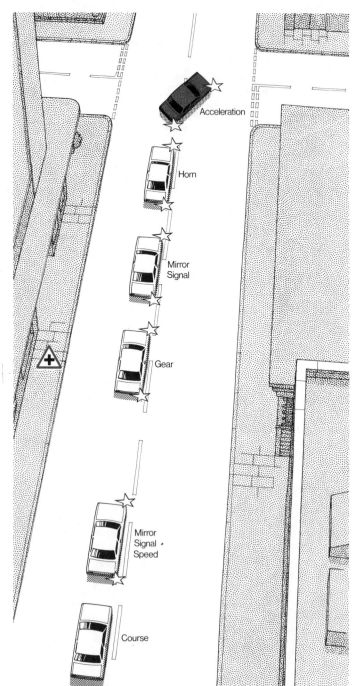

Acceleration

Horn

Mirror
Signal

Gear

Mirror
Signal
Speed

Course

Figure 1

mirrors and consider the need for signals bearing in mind that he may have to apply his brakes and that other road users in front and behind should be informed of his intention to slow down and turn right. (The signal given at feature one may, of course, still be operating). In the application of this feature the driver should aim to lose all unwanted road speed by braking, except for minor variations in speed when deceleration will be sufficient. If conditions on the approach to the hazard remain unchanged, no further braking should be necessary.

Feature Three—Gear

17 The gear selected should be appropriate to the road speed and one in which the vehicle will respond readily to variations of accelerator pressure. Final adjustments to speed may be made in this way. With automatic transmission the correct gear for the speed will not normally require any action by the driver.

Feature Four—Mirrors and Signals

18 Immediately after the gear change the driver should again use his mirrors to check the movement and position of following traffic, which may make it unsafe to turn. He should consider whether to now give a signal of his intention to deviate or whether an existing trafficator signal needs to be confirmed by arm.

Feature Five—Horn

19 No hard and fast rules can be laid down as to whether or not a horn warning should be sounded. The driver must be guided entirely by the circumstances, bearing in mind the need to make his presence known to other road users.

Feature Six—Acceleration

20 As he nears the junction the driver must consider the degree of acceleration required for the turn to be completed safely. Until the vehicle has passed through the apex of the curve the speed as determined at feature two will be maintained, with the engine pulling but without an increase of road speed. This will ensure best possible stability and reduce the effects of forces acting on a turning vehicle. After the apex the driver may accelerate but the point at which this will occur must be related to the type of road surface and its condition. On a good dry surface acceleration may be applied just after the apex with a gradual increase as the path of the vehicle straightens out. If the road surface is poor acceleration may have to be delayed until the vehicle resumes a straight course.

LEFT TURN (see figure 2)

Feature One—Course

21 The ideal course is well to the left of the road requiring little or no deviation from the driver's normal safety position. The mirrors must be used and if circumstances require a change of position, a deviation signal considered before altering course.

Feature Two—Mirrors, Signals and Speed

22 The mirrors must be used and deviation and slowing down signals considered before reducing speed. A turn to the left is normally slower than a right turn and the System will need to be started earlier.

Feature Three—Gear

23 The gear selected should be the most responsive for the speed at which the vehicle is being driven.

Feature Four—Mirrors and Signals

24 Immediately after the gear change the driver should again use his mirrors and decide whether it is still safe to turn left. He should also consider whether a left turn signal is necessary or whether an arm signal is required to emphasise a trafficator signal previously given.

Feature Five—Horn

25 Once again the driver must be guided by the circumstances (with particular consideration for pedestrians).

Feature Six—Acceleration

26 The driver must now consider the condition of the road surface in order to apply the correct degree of acceleration for the turn.

STRAIGHT AHEAD AT CROSSROADS

Feature One—Course

27 The adoption of the correct course on the approach is of paramount importance as it will vary with the type of junction. The driver must take into account the need to obtain a clear view into the roads to the right and left, the position of other traffic, the presence of stationary vehicles, lane markings and all other circumstances before deciding on the best course.

Figure 2

However, he must use the mirrors and, before any change of position is made, ensure that no danger or inconvenience is caused to others. A deviation signal would rarely be given as it would tend to confuse or mislead others as to his real intentions.

Feature Two—Mirrors, Signals and Speed

28 With the vehicle in the right position the driver must assess, in relation to what he can see, the correct speed to negotiate the hazard. It cannot be stressed too strongly that the speed is related directly to the view available into the roads to the right and left. The more restricted the view the slower the speed. He should use his mirrors and if it is necessary to reduce speed, consider a slowing down signal.

Feature Three—Gear

29 The correct gear must now be engaged for the road speed. This will enable the driver to accelerate out of the hazard if it is safe to do so, or stop more readily, if necessary.

Feature Four—Mirrors and Signals

30 The mirrors should again be used to note the position of following traffic but as the intention is to go straight on a deviation signal would not of course, be required.

Feature Five—Horn

31 The driver must assess the conditions and consider sounding the horn but it must not be used in the belief that it will ensure a safe passage.

Feature Six—Acceleration

32 Acceleration may be applied to drive the vehicle out of the hazard once the driver is satisfied that he can safely continue.

ROUNDABOUTS

33 Roundabouts assist traffic flow at junctions by allowing traffic to enter and leave by different roads with the minimum of inconvenience or danger. They are one way systems in which traffic circulates in a clockwise direction and vary in size and shape from the 'mini' roundabout to the large gyratory complex. The System of Car Control on the approach will be concerned with entering the roundabout. The general rule is to give way to traffic from the immediate right but to keep moving if the way is clear. Road markings may indicate otherwise.

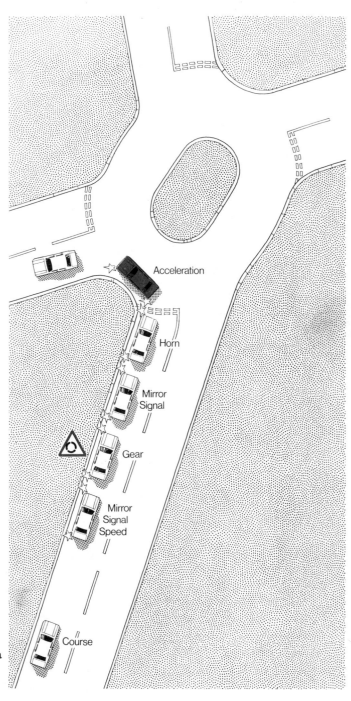

Figure 3a

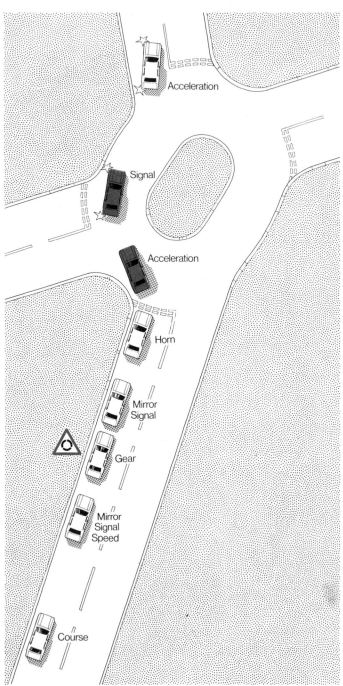

Figure 3b

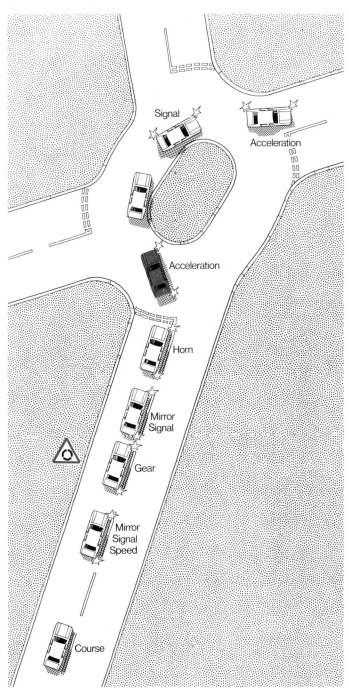

Figure 3c

Feature One—Course
34 The course selected will depend upon the intended direction of travel and the presence of other road users.
Where there is no other traffic following or in the vicinity and route directions permit, the best course is the shortest distance between the entrance and exit. Otherwise the course selected should be as follows:

(a) TURNING LEFT—Position on the approach should be in the nearside keeping to that position in the roundabout. (See figure 3a).

(b) STRAIGHT AHEAD—Position on the approach should be in the nearside unless conditions dictate otherwise. The chosen lane should be maintained through the roundabout. (See figure 3b).

(c) TURNING RIGHT—Position on the approach should be to the offside keeping to that position in the roundabout. (See figure 3c).
The mirrors must be used before the course is selected and any necessary signal given.

Feature Two—Mirrors, Signals and Speed
35 It will normally be necessary to slow down for the roundabout having due regard to the need to give way to traffic from the immediate right. The mirrors must be used and a slow down signal given if required. If intending to turn left or right a trafficator signal must also be considered and maintained through the roundabout.

Feature Three—Gear
36 The most responsive gear for the speed of the vehicle should now be selected.

Feature Four—Mirrors and Signals
37 Immediately after the gear change the driver should use the mirrors to check the situation behind. Directional signals should be considered at this stage if not previously given at Feature Two.

Feature Five—Horn
38 The use of the horn must now be considered.

Feature Six—Acceleration
39 Before turning into the roundabout acceleration is considered but generally the contours of the roads and the close

proximity of other hazards will render an increase of speed undesirable.

Negotiating the Roundabout

40 The hazards presented by the road layout and the movement of other vehicles must be dealt with as they arise by using the appropriate features of the System. A left trafficator signal should be considered when opposite the junction before the one by which it is intended to leave. Acceleration to leave the roundabout should be applied as for a left turn.

CHILDREN PLAYING ON NEARSIDE FOOTPATH

Feature One—Course

41 The course selected should be one which gives the greatest possible margin of safety in relation to the children, i.e. a position further towards the crown of the road than the normal safety position, but having regard to oncoming traffic.

The mirrors must be used and by early and gradual deviation the correct position adopted. A deviation signal would rarely be given because it may well mislead other road users, particularly following drivers who may interpret it incorrectly and attempt to overtake on the nearside.

Feature Two—Mirrors, Signals and Speed

42 The mirrors will again be used. Assessment of a safe speed for this hazard will depend on a number of factors, including how close it will be necessary to go to the children, the possibility that one or more of them may run into the road, the road surface, etc. A major reduction in speed by braking may possibly require a slowing down signal but a deviation signal would not be given.

Feature Three—Gear

43 Whether or not speed has been reduced a lower gear may be required to give flexibility for that speed.

Feature Four—Mirrors and Signals

44 The mirrors should again be used but no signals given.

Feature Five—Horn

45 The less the distance between the vehicle and the children the more likely the need for a horn warning. This should be given early so they have time to react. Children are unpredictable and the giving of a horn warning does not guarantee the driver a safe passage through the hazard.

Feature Six—Acceleration

46 Once the driver is satisfied that he can continue normally he may accelerate away.

47 It will be seen from the examples given that the System of Car Control is used on the approach to all hazards although every feature may not, in fact, be applied. Once the driver has learned the System he should practise it continually. He will find through experience that circumstances may alter on the approach to a hazard calling for a change of driving plan. The application of the System will become instinctive and form the basis upon which the finer points of driving can be built.

CHAPTER 2

ACCELERATION, GEAR CHANGING, BRAKING AND STEERING

Acceleration

1 A thorough understanding of the System of Car Control coupled with intelligent use of the accelerator, gears, brakes and steering is essential if the expertise associated with a skilled driver is to be developed.

2 'Acceleration' in this context means an increase of road speed of a motor vehicle when pressure is exerted by the driver on the accelerator pedal. Conversely, speed may be reduced when pressure on the pedal is eased.

3 The acceleration capabilities of different vehicles vary considerably according to the efficiency of the engine and the power to weight ratio. An engine will respond to increased pressure on the accelerator only if it can develop the power to do the work demanded. All references to acceleration will assume that the correct gear is engaged and that the desired road speed is safe.

4 A good driver will use the accelerator pedal precisely avoiding sudden and coarse movements which result in uneven acceleration. The accelerator pedal is spring loaded to its closed position and the driver must accustom himself to the tension if he is to operate it smoothly. A defect or incorrect adjustment in the mechanical linkage between the pedal and the carburetter may defeat accurate control. Thin soled shoes are preferable if delicate control is to be achieved.

The Behaviour of a Car under the Influence of Acceleration

5 Acceleration affects the behaviour of a vehicle as it travels along the road. Figure 4 shows that, when under the influence of acceleration, a vehicle tends to settle down on to the road at the rear improving the grip of the tyres on the road surface. This is a desirable condition when accelerating on the straight but care should be taken when driving through a curved path. The vehicle is most stable when the weight is evenly distributed, the engine just pulling with no increase in road speed.

Acceleration Sense

6 This is the ability of the driver to vary the speed of the vehicle by accurate use of the accelerator to meet changing road and

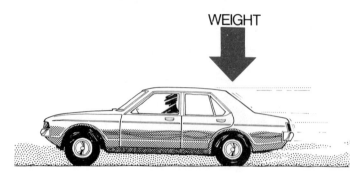

WEIGHT

Figure 4

traffic conditions. Acceleration sense can be applied to every facet of driving, e.g. following other vehicles, overtaking, approaching hazards and changes in road features. The essence is good observation coupled with sound judgment of speed and distance.

7 Lack of acceleration sense is often associated with applying acceleration to leave a hazard when it should have been obvious that braking would be demanded for a traffic hold up ahead.

8 Similarly some drivers maintain speed too long when coming up behind a slower moving vehicle and find it necessary to brake and wait momentarily before overtaking. A more skilled driver would have eased off a little earlier by using acceleration sense and approached and passed the vehicle at a constant speed.

9 The object of Feature Six in the System of Car Control is to accelerate safely out of the hazard with due regard for the nature of the road surface.

10 The correct degree of acceleration in relation to the surface is important at all times but becomes more critical when the vehicle is driven through a curved path. At the commencement of the curve the vehicle must be travelling at the correct speed which should remain constant until the apex has been passed. It must be appreciated that when a vehicle is turning it will be necessary to increase power if the same speed is to be maintained. The point at which acceleration is commenced, and the amount applied, will depend on the state of the road surface. As conditions deteriorate it may be necessary to wait until the vehicle resumes a straight course. By following this method of negotiating a curve the vehicle will always remain in a condition of maximum possible stability.

Gear Changing

11 Effective acceleration is possible only when a useful and economical increase in engine revolutions is obtainable. The use of the gearbox must therefore be considered in conjunction with the capabilities of the vehicle.

12 One of the hallmarks of a good driver is the ability to change gear smoothly and make the best use of the gear ratios of the vehicle he is driving. To this end the use of the double de-clutch method of changing gear may be beneficial.

13 The driver's judgment of the correct use of the gears available to him will improve if he has a good knowledge of the main components of the gearbox and their functions.

14 No matter how well a driver may handle a vehicle, his use of the gearbox will do much to make or mar his driving. The essential ingredients are the ability to accurately match engine revolutions to road speed together with precise operation of clutch, accelerator and gears. The first class driver should aim always:

(a) To be in the correct gear for every road speed and traffic situation.

(b) To make all gear changes quietly and smoothly.

(c) To be capable of engaging a particular gear without first using an intermediate gear.

(d) To know the approximate maximum road speed in each gear of the vehicle he is driving.

Moving from Stationary

15 If the gearbox and clutch are skilfully used a vehicle will be put into motion smoothly and its speed increased progressively by the use of higher gear ratios. Maximum acceleration through the gears will be necessary only on rare occasions of pressing need. Care must be taken not to 'over rev' in the lower gears nor to remain in a gear beyond the limits of its optimum performance.

Changing Down

16 When the speed of a vehicle is reduced by a gradient, for traffic conditions or other hazards, a lower gear may be needed. A driver must develop his judgment of when to change to a lower gear.

17 A lower gear will be selected for one of two reasons:

(a) loss of road speed to within the range of the next lower gear despite continued pressure on the accelerator pedal, and

(b) on the approach to a hazard when a more responsive gear is required.

18 The selection of a suitable lower gear at the correct time will provide advantages in the following circumstances:

(a) On an up gradient; to maintain the power to climb the hill.

(b) On a steep down gradient; to control speed with engine compression, thereby avoiding long periods of hard braking.

(c) At the approach to a hazard; to enable the driver to accelerate out of the hazard, if this is safe, or to stop more readily if necessary.

(d) When travelling at low speeds or when in doubt about traffic conditions ahead, to provide the reserve of power and flexibility to accelerate or decelerate by control through the accelerator pedal.

(e) On a slippery road; when the use of engine compression to lose speed is safer than braking, since the latter would be liable to cause skidding.

Faults

19 Common faults relating to the use of gears are:

(a) Poor co-ordination between foot and hand to effect a clean, smooth gear change.

(b) Inability to recognise by the sound of the engine when a gear change is required.

(c) Failure to select the correct gear for the existing road speed.

(d) Changing to a lower gear on a "closing gap", e.g. inadequate braking followed by a gear change and hurried re-application of brakes.

(e) Changing down instead of braking (other than in the circumstances shown in paragraph 18e).

(f) Failure to take a proper grip on the gear lever when moving it from one position to another. This is the root of many gear changing difficulties.

(g) Late gear changing, or entire failure to change down, at the approach to a hazard when the road speed and conditions demand a lower gear.

(h) Failure to match engine revolutions to road speed when changing down.

(i) Timidity and reluctance to attempt necessary changes down to low gears.

20 Some common faults when driving vehicles fitted with automatic transmission are:

(a) Failure to ensure brakes are 'ON' before engaging 'D' or 'R' from stationary.

(b) Engaging 'D' or 'R' with a high revving engine (often associated with use of choke).

(c) Engaging lower gear 'hold' at too high a road speed.

(d) Moving the selector to 'N' when making temporary stops in traffic.

(e) Braking with the left foot (except when manoeuvring at low speed).

21 Car sympathy is a quality to be developed in many ways, not the least of which is gear changing. The driver who demonstrates delicacy and smoothness in his gear changing will be on the way to acquiring that polished style which is the ultimate aim.

Braking

22 More important than being able to accelerate and change gear is the ability to slow down or stop the vehicle when required. There are two ways in which this may be done:

(a) by deceleration as the pressure on the accelerator pedal is relaxed, or

(b) by the application of the brakes.

23 When pressure on the accelerator pedal is relaxed, the engine will slow down due to the compression in the cylinders and this slowing down will be transmitted to the wheels. Thus the engine is acting as a brake and the reduction of speed will be smooth and gradual with little wear to the vehicle.

24 The loss of road speed by engine deceleration will be more pronounced when a low gear is engaged, including an automatic gearbox. This will be valuable when driving on slippery roads when normal braking could lock the wheels or where making long descents in hilly country but for normal driving requirements it is inefficient other than for minor variations in speed.

25 For normal driving a more efficient method of slowing down than relying on engine deceleration is to apply the brakes. Pressure on the footbrake pedal can be varied at the discretion of the driver from a barely perceptible effect to such force that all wheels will lock. For all normal braking the initial free movement of the pedal should be taken up gently and pressure progressively increased as necessary until it can be relaxed as the unwanted road speed is lost. When braking to a standstill the final effort should be so judged that the vehicle is brought to a gliding halt without jerking or settling down suddenly at the rear end.

26 Apart from other considerations the speed of a vehicle at any time must not exceed the speed at which it can be stopped within the distance the driver can see to be clear. The driver must know the distance he needs to slow down appreciably or stop from all road speeds. Not only must he know the distances he must be able to relate them to the road on which he is travelling. On a good dry road the average vehicle should be capable of stopping in the following distances:

Speed in m.p.h.	Speed in ft/sec	Braking distance in feet
30	44	45
45	66	101
60	88	180
90	132	405

These distances will, of course, increase considerably in wet or slippery conditions. (A guide to the braking distance of a vehicle in feet may be found by squaring the speed in m.p.h. and dividing by 20.)

27 To the braking distance must be added the distance travelled in the driver's reaction time to arrive at an overall stopping distance. Reaction time may be defined as the time that passes between the moment the driver observes the need for action and the moment he takes that action. The average driver takes 0·7 seconds from seeing an emergency situation to placing his foot on the brake pedal. The distance covered in that time is known as the "thinking distance" and will be the same figure in feet as the speed in m.p.h., e.g. 30 m.p.h. = 30 feet. Thinking distance + braking distance = stopping distance.

28 The thinking distance will vary in three ways:

(a) With the speed of the vehicle.

(b) With the physical and mental condition of the driver.

(c) With the degree of concentration being applied.

29 Controlled, progressive braking is preferable to a sudden hard application. Figure 5 illustrates the behaviour of a moving car under the influence of braking. The weight is thrown forward and downward on to the front wheels and the rear tends to lift. The resulting unequal distribution of weight makes the steering heavier and reduces the general stability of the car, especially at the rear wheels. This effect can be dangerous, particularly when the vehicle is travelling on a curved path.

Figure 5

30 To reduce these disadvantages as much as possible the following rules for braking should be applied:

(1) Brake firmly only when travelling in a straight line.

(2) Brake in plenty of time.

(3) Vary brake pressure according to the condition of the road surface.

(4) When descending a steep winding hill brake firmly on the straight stretches and ease off in the bends. Remember the value of engaging a low gear at an early stage in the descent.

Braking under Normal Traffic Conditions

31 Loss of roadspeed on the approach to a hazard is Feature Two of the System of Car Control. Having observed the nature of the hazard and selected the appropriate course (Feature One), the brakes will be applied as necessary to lose speed. When to apply the brakes and the pedal pressure required will depend upon the initial speed, the road surface and the assessment of a safe speed for the hazard as it is approached. Braking may need to be firm but should never be fierce. The loss of speed should be constant and steady from the first movement of the brake pedal to the point where the speed is right to enter the hazard; neither too early, so that it becomes necessary to accelerate towards the hazard, nor too late, so that a late and forceful application becomes necessary.

Emergency Braking—Good Dry Road

32 Brake design enables the driver to vary his effort on the brake pedal to the extent that he can lock the road wheels if he wishes. The brakes are most effective when the wheel is still revolving just before it locks and devices can be fitted to most vehicles which prevent the brakes being applied beyond maximum efficiency whatever extra pressure is exerted by the driver. Unfortunately no driver can match the sensitivity of the brake limiter systems and the quickest stopping distance on a good dry road will be achieved by applying the brakes as hard as possible to skid to a stop in a straight line. Note the qualification as to stopping in a straight line. The driver must quickly assess at the time whether he has room in which to brake to a standstill on a straight course or whether he should relax the brake pressure to steer out of trouble.

Emergency Braking—Slippery Road

33 On slippery surfaces, particularly when a four wheel skid has occurred, the vehicle can be stopped in a shorter distance by resorting to cadence braking. The word 'cadence' means with rhythm. Hence cadence braking consists of a succession of rhythmic pumps on the brake pedal. The brakes of any vehicle being at their most effective when they are on the point of locking up, it necessarily follows that each time the brake is pumped hard and the wheels lock, maximum braking effect must have taken place. The harder the brakes are pumped the better the effect, so no finesse is required in operation, thus making the technique easy for even inexperienced drivers. It is necessary for the driver to pump with deliberation rather than speed and to pause momentarily at the full extent of brake pedal travel and not to 'bounce' the foot on and off the pedal. Pausing at the full extent of brake pedal travel will allow as much as possible of the weight of the vehicle to be transferred to the front. When the brake is released ready for the next pump, the front suspension having absorbed the weight allows the front of the vehicle to rise. By pumping rhythmically more and more weight is thrown forward on to the front wheels reducing the tendency for them to lock and slide. Better braking effect is thus achieved and directional control retained.

Brake Test

34 The correct operation of the brakes is vital to proper control of a vehicle. A driver should check the movement of the hand and foot controls when he first enters the car and, as soon as possible after moving off, test the foot brake under running conditions. This test should ideally be carried out at a speed of 30 m.p.h. in top gear on a level stretch of road with a good surface but it may be necessary to compromise in some respects. The object of the test is to see how the vehicle responds to a normal application of the brakes when applied firmly and progressively. The vehicle should pull up on a straight course without swerving to either side and with even braking to all wheels. When speed has been reduced to 15 m.p.h. the brakes can be eased off and re-applied sharply to check the operation of some inertia seat belts.

DUE REGARD MUST BE GIVEN TO THE SAFETY AND CONVENIENCE OF OTHER ROAD USERS.

Hand Brake

35 Unless there is a failure of the foot brake the hand brake should not be applied until the vehicle is stationary. It should then be applied with the pawl release operated to prevent wear to the ratchet. Inexperienced drivers should apply the hand brake whenever the vehicle is brought to rest during a journey but as experience is gained it will not be necessary for every momentary stop. As to stopping and leaving the vehicle —see Chapter 10 paragraph 3.

Steering

36 A modern motor vehicle in good order will keep to a straight course on a straight and level road with little or no steering control by the driver. On cambered roads a vehicle will tend to run down the camber but very little movement of the steering wheel will be needed to compensate. It is not until a vehicle is directed into a curved path that precise steering presents any difficulty.

37 Different makes and types of vehicle have different steering characteristics built-in as design features. Steering may be light or heavy; the vehicle may respond more (oversteer) or less (understeer) than the driver anticipates; the steering movement may be power assisted. The driver must quickly adapt himself to the characteristics of the vehicle he is driving so that he is able to place it where he wants it under all conditions.

38 Accurate steering depends to a large extent upon the way in which the driver sits in the vehicle and holds the wheel. The seat should be adjusted so that the pedals can be operated and the hand controls are within reach but not so close to the wheel that movement of the arms is restricted. For best control he should be upright and alert; not taut or strained, yet not too relaxed; nor concerned primarily with comfort.

39 The hands should be placed naturally with the palms on the rim of the wheel just above the half way position. The hands on the wheel will be in the same position as the hands on a clock when the time is ten minutes to two. Fingers should fold around the rim, resting lightly but ready to grip when necessary. Any emergency movement of the wheel can be done immediately by either hand as required.

40 Both hands should remain on the wheel unless it is necessary to remove one or other to signal, operate an auxiliary switch or to change gear, etc. Any change from the straight course must be accomplished gradually and smoothly other than when manoeuvring at slow speeds.

41 Minor variations in course calling for up to an inch or so of steering wheel movement, e.g. changing traffic lanes, will not normally require the hands to be moved from their basic positions on the wheel. For more positive steering operations the hands should move as described below. For the sake of simplicity steering to the left is described, although the same method is applied for left or right deviations (see figure 6).

(a) When intending to turn to the left the left hand should be moved to a higher position on the wheel.

(b) The initial steering effort is to pull down with the left hand. If the movement of the left hand down to its initial position is sufficient to turn the vehicle into the desired path the right hand remains motionless and allows the rim to slide through.

(c) If the steering imparted by the left hand moving to its original level is insufficient to negotiate the turn the right hand should slide down the wheel keeping level with the left hand as it pulls down. When the left hand has pulled the wheel down the right hand grips the rim and pushes upwards. The left hand moves up level with it, allowing the rim to slide through the fingers.

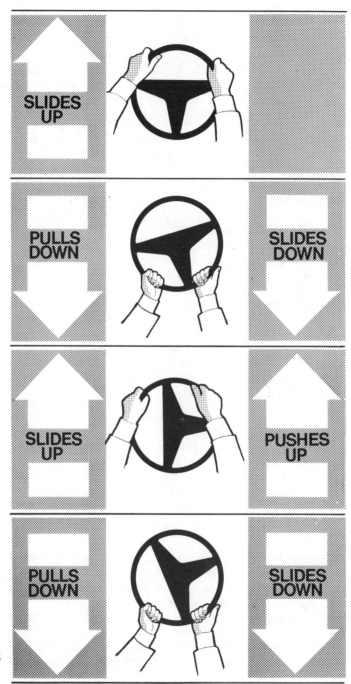

Figure 6

(d) Movements (a) to (c) will be repeated until the desired turn is achieved.

For a turn to the right the same method is used but the first steering movement will be the right hand pulling down and so on as described above. Each hand should be kept to its own side of the wheel and not pass the 12 O'Clock position.

42 Having turned the vehicle sufficiently it must be straightened or it will continue in a circular path. Most vehicles have steering which is self straightening and control will be necessary to prevent the steering wheel from spinning back. Accordingly, the steering wheel should be fed back by hand movements similar to those in paragraph 41 but in the reverse direction.

Steering when Manoeuvring

43 It is possible, particularly in a vehicle fitted with power assisted steering, for sufficient effort to be exerted on the steering wheel to move the road wheels when the vehicle is stationary. This practice should be avoided because of the strain imposed on the steering linkage. Steering effort should not be applied unless the vehicle is moving, albeit extremely slowly. Manoeuvring a vehicle in a confined space demands very slow speeds and large, rapid movements of the steering wheel. The push pull steering method will give effective steering when moving forward or backward but sometimes for reversing a different hold will be preferred.

44 When reversing one hand placed at the top of the steering wheel will often give adequate control. The other hand may adopt a low position, either with a loose hold allowing the wheel to slide through it, or to hold the wheel in position whilst a new grip is taken at the top. The driver must look over his right or left shoulder to see where he is going but the view to the left may be improved by turning the body and placing the left arm on the back of the seat. The seat belt may be undone if it restricts movement.

45 Manoeuvring into or out of a confined space may need more than one movement forward or backward. In these circumstances the steering wheel should be turned rapidly in the appropriate direction as the vehicle starts to move, held on full lock for as long as possible and turned back the opposite way at the last moment before the vehicle is stopped. When the vehicle starts off on the next leg of the manoeuvre the front wheels will be pointing in the right direction. (See also Hints on Reversing, Chapter 10 paragraph 4).

Rules for Steering
46

(1) Elbows are not to be placed on the window frame, arm rests, etc., this reduces control and looks slack.

(2) Hands should be placed on the wheel in the 'ten to two' position, not gripping tightly but ready to exert maximum leverage if necessary.

(3) The grip should be tightened when cornering or braking, both hands holding the wheel during these operations.

(4) On slippery roads steering movements should be delicate or skids may be induced.

47 Poor road observation or inadequate planning may result in effective steering control being difficult to maintain. Steering cannot be precise if the brakes are on or if the speed is too high for the manoeuvre. It therefore follows that good observation and intelligent use of the System of Car Control are essential if these difficulties are to be avoided.

CHAPTER 3

DRIVERS' SIGNALS

1 Signals are the means by which drivers warn other road users of their intentions and presence. They are the language of the road. If they are to be understood they must be as illustrated in the Highway Code. To be of any use they must be given clearly and in good time.

2 Signals are informative in that they may give notice of an intention to carry out a manoeuvre. They give a warning not an instruction and give no right whatsoever to carry out the intended action unless it is safe.

3 Drivers' signals are divided for the purposes of this chapter into the categories shown below:

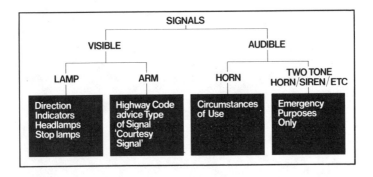

VISIBLE SIGNALS

Lamp
5 The meaning of the direction indicator signals illustrated in the Highway Code are as follows:
    (a) I intend to move out to the right or turn right.
    (b) I intend to move in to the left or turn left or stop on the left.

6 Care should be taken when the left indicator is used as a signal for stopping on the nearside just past a junction on the left. This could be misleading, as, for example, a driver waiting in the road on the left may move out, thinking that the approaching vehicle is going to turn left.

7 A common fault is that of leaving the indicator in operation long after the turn has been completed. It follows that a driver waiting to emerge from a side turning should not accept an indicator signal as complete proof of another driver's intention. He should wait for supporting evidence, e.g. a considerable reduction in speed, before moving out.

8 Another form of signalling by lamp is that of flashing the headlights during the hours of darkness. This is an effective means of giving warning of approach to a road junction or to a driver before overtaking him. The headlights should be used in good time for junctions but other road users must not be dazzled. (See also Chapter 4 paras 37-45).

9 The flashing of headlights should not be used for signalling in daylight unless in lieu of a horn warning for overtaking at speed on motorways, dual carriageways, and other fast roads when the System and, therefore, the warning of approach will be earlier than on other types of roads. The length of the warning will be determined by the circumstances existing at the time but in any case should consist of only one flash. The use of this form of signalling during the day calls for care as it is becoming the practice for many drivers to interpret a headlamp flash as an invitation to take precedence.

10 The stop lamps fitted to the rear of the vehicle and operating with the foot brake pedal are a useful form of signal but they do not work until the brakes are applied. In circumstances where advance warning should be given of the intention to slow down or stop, e.g. at a pedestrian crossing, the arm signal should be used.

Arm
11 The Highway Code illustrates the arm signals to be given when indicators or stop lights are faulty. Such signals should also be given to emphasise an intention or to confirm a mechanical signal already given. The signals are as follows:

(a) 'I intend to move out to the right or turn right'. The palm of the hand faces the front, fingers extended and close together.

(b) 'I intend to move in to the left or turn left'. The arm is slowly rotated in an anti-clockwise direction with a flexed elbow, the palm of the hand facing the front.

(c) 'I intend to slow down or stop'. The palm of the hand, with fingers extended and close together, faces the ground. The arm is slowly lowered and raised several times.

In each case the arm should be extended as far as possible remaining outside the car for not less than three seconds.

12 The expert driver will not only give exemplary signals himself but will also know the signals given by other road users. Signals to go ahead given by unauthorised persons must not be relied upon but a signal to stop given by anybody should be treated with due respect in the interests of safety. There may have been an accident, etc.

13 It is appropriate here to include a mention of the courtesy signal, i.e. an acknowledgement of a courtesy extended by another road user by raising the hand. It should not be overdone nor should it be neglected for its general use can do much to promote good road manners.

14 Visible signals should always be linked with mirrors. 'Mirrors and Signals' will become a habit and ensure that necessary signals are given to following traffic.

AUDIBLE SIGNALS

Horn
15 The horn should be sounded only when it is really necessary. No hard and fast rules can be laid down but there are certain occasions when the use of the horn is justified even though every other precaution has been taken.

(a) To attract the attention of another road user who is obviously vulnerable. Pedestrians and cyclists, particularly children, are usually involved.

(b) When approaching a hazard where the view is very limited, such as a blind bend.

(c) Prior to overtaking, bearing in mind the following:

(i) Is the driver in front aware he is about to be overtaken.

(ii) Can he be given plenty of room in case he should deviate slightly.

(iii) Will unexpected overtaking at speed be likely to disturb him.

16 Experience, intuition and the possibility of adopting an alternative driving plan must be the criteria upon which a driver decides to sound, or not to sound, the horn. In heavy traffic occasions for using the horn are rare, primarily because speeds are moderate and other action can be taken in good time.

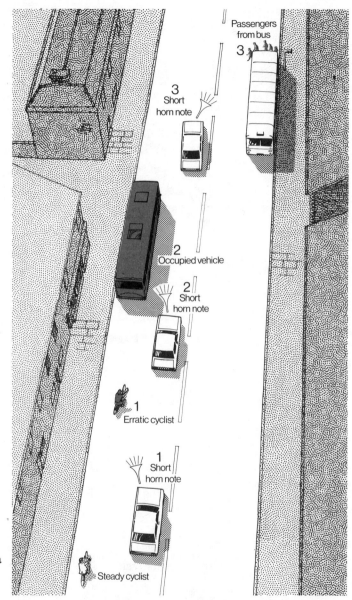

Figure 7a

17 The horn warning should be confined as far as possible to one note, either short or long, according to traffic conditions and the type of road user for whom it is sounded. Figures 7a and b show some common occasions for the use of the short or long note.

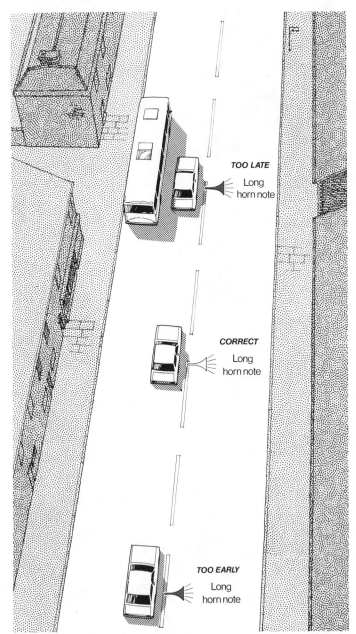

Figure 7b

18 Horns should not be sounded in an aggressive or demanding manner, but always courteously, giving plenty of time for other road users to react.

Two Tone Horns/Sirens, etc.

19 Two tone horns, sirens, etc., are fitted to police vehicles for use when a police driver engaged upon an urgent assignment is being impeded and needs to obtain a clear passage through traffic. Most drivers on hearing the warning of an approaching emergency service vehicle will endeavour to allow precedence to it but the police driver must understand that the use of the warning instrument gives him NO PROTECTION OR RIGHT OF WAY WHATSOEVER. He must never drive at a speed faster than is safe for the conditions nor other than in accordance with the instructions in this manual. His duty to the public generally, his crew and himself is quite clear in this respect.

CHAPTER 4

ROAD OBSERVATION

1 The object of this chapter is to assist the driver to improve his standard of road observation by considering individual aspects of the subject.

Concentration
2 Good vision, hearing and standard of health all have a bearing on the amount of concentration which can be given to any activity at any one time.

3 The ability to concentrate exists in everyone but few can concentrate sufficiently to drive a motor car with complete mastery for very long. The driver must therefore adjust the speed of his vehicle to the degree of concentration he is able to apply at the time. Without self discipline attention is inclined to wander from essential points of observation. A conscious effort must be made to prevent this.

4 Concentration and Road Observation are very closely related, for without the former, success in the latter cannot possibly be achieved. It is not enough merely to see every detail in a road scene; the value of what is seen must be assessed and upon that value, a driving plan formulated. Concentration and therefore road observation will improve if a driver comments out loud on what he sees and what he intends to do.

Driving Plans
5 Driving plans should be made on the correct assessment of the ever changing scene ahead and to the rear of the vehicle. The driver should be able to make driving decisions without hesitation in a methodical manner at any moment. All decisions must be based on the principle of safety for others as well as himself.

6 Driving plans and decisions are made on a combination of:

(a) What can be seen.

(b) What cannot be seen.

(c) The circumstances which may reasonably be expected to develop.

Decisions can rarely be based solely on (a) because there are many stretches of road where the layout and traffic conditions do not permit an unobstructed view. The greatest difficulties arise from areas into which the driver cannot see, such as around bends and corners, behind trees and buildings, at places where roads converge or where other traffic obstructs the view of the road beyond. In these circumstances in particular the driver must be able to stop his vehicle in the distance he can see to be clear.

7 Allowances should always be made for the mistakes of other road users. It is unsafe to assume that another driver will react correctly to any given situation; he may have passed his test only that day or be driving a strange or defective vehicle. He may be naturally aggressive or thoughtless or attempting to drive beyond his capabilities to keep an urgent appointment. Driving to the System will prevent a driver from becoming involved in an accident for which he is directly responsible. By concentration, early recognition of potential danger and a defensive attitude of mind he will also avoid accidents which could result from the mistakes of others.

8 Driving plans, therefore, must be based upon what is actually observed, the assumption that there may be danger in every obscured section of road and that others may do something foolish at any moment.

View from the Vehicle
9 The driver must aim to have the best possible view around the vehicle at all times. This can only be achieved by ensuring that the windscreen and other windows are kept clean inside and out, that windscreen wipers and washers are in good working order and the mirrors always properly adjusted. Before wipers are switched on the washers should be used to assist in cleaning particles of dust and grit from the screen which might otherwise cause damage.

10 The design of the vehicle may restrict the driver's view in some areas and he should move to look around any obstruction. When reversing, a pedestrian or obstruction to the rear can be obscured by the body-work of the vehicle. Extra precautions are therefore essential before beginning the manoeuvre.

How Vision is Affected by Speed
11 Crowds of pedestrians can move about on the pavements without colliding with one another, not so much because they are looking out for obstructions, but mainly because their speed of movement is so slow that they can change their pace and

direction in time to avoid collision. If, however, one of them wishes to get along quickly he has to look farther ahead and vary his course and speed accordingly. He then finds that his view of other pedestrians at close quarters deteriorates, so that quite often, if one of them comes into his path suddenly, they may collide.

12 The driver of a vehicle adjusts the length and breadth of his vision in a similar way, but of course, over greater distances. As speed increases so his focal point must be moved farther ahead for objects there to appear clear and well defined. Objects in the foreground become less distinct.

13 When road speed must be kept low because of traffic conditions the focal point needs to be closer for the driver to observe foreground details. These often indicate that a dangerous situation is developing and he then has time, owing to his low speed, to take precautions which will prevent him from becoming involved.

14 The driver must therefore focus his eyes according to speed and when there are many foreground details to be seen speed must be kept low if collisions are to be avoided. It is clearly dangerous to drive fast in the wrong places.

15 Continuous driving for long periods may result in fatigue which will cause eye strain and lack of concentration. Although special efforts may be made by the driver to maintain his normal standard of observation he will find that the task becomes increasingly difficult. His recognition and assessments of dangerous situations will become late and inaccurate.

Weather Conditions

16 Weather conditions such as fog, mist, heavy rain or snow, the fading daylight and bright sunshine reduce visibility considerably. To meet these conditions speed must be reduced so that objects in the immediate foreground may be seen in time to take any necessary action.

17 In daylight fog or conditions of poor visibility headlamps must be switched on. Where there is fog or falling snow at night fog lamps should be used as an alternative to, or in conjunction with, dipped headlamps. Adapt the choice of lights to the conditions. A clearer view may be obtained by the use of windscreen washers and wipers. A slow steady pace should be maintained using the edge of the carriageway, hazard lines and reflective studs (cats eyes) as a guide especially when approaching a road junction or corner. Be prepared for sudden stoppages of traffic ahead and do not follow too closely.

Traffic should be overtaken only when it is absolutely safe and will seldom be possible in fog on a two way road.

Road Surfaces

18 The average motorist is not so well acquainted with the road surface types and conditions as he should be. It is useless to complain about a slippery surface after a skid has occurred. A good driver is the one who looks well ahead, recognises any change in road surface conditions and then applies correct values of braking, acceleration and steering so that maximum road holding is always achieved.

19 When clean and dry the surfaces of most properly made up roads are good or fairly good for road holding. In wet weather they may become slippery, particularly during a shower of rain following a long spell of dry weather. The presence of snow, frost, ice, oil, moist muddy patches or wet leaves, dry loose dust or gravel, etc., can cause tyres to lose adhesion.

20 The adverse surfaces mentioned in para. 19 are all recognisable and they have their own distinctive appearances. Unfortunately, these conditions are frequently found at the approach to, or at, hazards where steering, braking and acceleration may need alteration and tyre adhesion is then of paramount importance.

21 Most roads have a surface of asphalt or other compounds which may have a dressing of stones or chips. These have a comparatively high non-skid value and are easily recognised. In time they take on a polished appearance and lose some of their non-skid properties.

22 Concrete road surfaces usually have a distinctive appearance, through being light in colour, some have a roughened formation of lateral ribs, most have a good non-skid value. Some, however, are apt to hold surface water which in cold weather freezes, creating a slippery surface which is not easily seen.

23 Wood blocks and stone setts are encountered occasionally in towns and cities. Great care must be taken when driving on these surfaces to avoid skidding, which will occur from the slightest cause, especially when wet.

24 During wintry weather, road surfaces become frost and ice covered, but not always uniformly. Isolated patches and certain gradients remain iced up when other parts have thawed out. The good driver should be on his look out for these areas and recognise them not only from their appearance

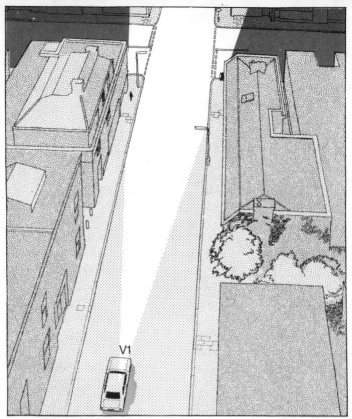

Figure 8a

Figure 8b

but from the behaviour of other vehicles, and will take due precautions in good time to avoid skidding. Remember, tyres travelling on ice make virtually no noise.

25 Wear and tear to the vehicle should be reduced so far as practicable by keeping a good look out for potholes, projecting man hole covers, sunken gullies and any material likely to damage tyres. To avoid these the course must be altered slightly if this can be done without inconvenience to other road users. If they cannot be avoided, speed must be reduced so that rough ground is traversed slowly, thus maintaining stability and reducing to a minimum the shock to the vehicle.

Road Signs and Markings

26 There are many road signs and markings and it is important for the information or directions they give to be understood. Every sign or road marking must be seen in good time if the driver is to comply with it or profit from the information given.

27 Having seen the sign and understood its meaning, the driver should look beyond it to the road layout or condition to which it refers. He will then have ample opportunity to assess the situation and formulate a safe driving plan.

28 It is disturbing but true that the average road user does not see and understand the majority of the signs provided for his guidance, unless he makes a conscious effort or is in search of specific information. Every driver should cultivate a special interest in and respect for all signs and markings; by so doing he will improve his road observation and general standard of road behaviour.

Zones of Visibility

29 The area ahead of the driver is divided into zones where his view is good and zones where his view is obstructed. It is essential when approaching areas of potential danger where view is restricted to make maximum use of all available aids so that driving may be planned accordingly.

30 Figure 8 illustrates a crossroads and the improving view available to the driver on his approach as he applies the features of the System. From V1 to V3 the view improves very little, which shows how necessary it is to approach the hazard with special care. From V4 the view into the converging roads rapidly improves, enabling the driver to make his decision to maintain or increase speed, slow down or stop, according to the position and behaviour of other road users.

31 The observant driver will take full advantage of open spaces and breaks in hedges, fences or walls, to get that valuable, if brief, view into converging roads which to some drivers appear totally obscured. It is often possible to judge the severity of any bend or gradient by the position, etc., of trees, hedges and other features. Figures 9a and b illustrate the zones at the approach to a crossroad where the view is restricted. The zone on the driver's right is broken up by gaps in the wall which runs alongside the road. View into the nearside converging road is at first quite poor, but the set back of the hedge at the actual junction provides a superior view at a later stage to that on the off-side, which becomes poor again owing to the presence of the wall.

32 The driver should also be aware of the limited view in relation to stationary and moving vehicles ahead which can be improved to some extent by early appreciation and correct positioning. This subject will be discussed more fully in Chapter 5. The main point to remember is that the closer a vehicle is to the one ahead the less the driver can see.

Aids to Good Road Observation

33 One of the most important aids to successful driving is local knowledge. To know the situation of main road junctions, one-way streets and roundabout systems is undoubtedly of great assistance to the driver but his driving plan for each hazard must be based on the prevailing conditions, rather than what is normally found there.

34 Town driving in particular demands complete concentration, road observation, the ability to react quickly to changing situations and considerable driving skill. Views ahead are frequently restricted owing to the density of the traffic. It is not wise to focus all one's attention on the vehicle immediately in front and a sensible distance should be maintained behind it so that a view of traffic movement two or three vehicles ahead is obtained from time to time.

35 In places where traffic is really heavy and slow, driving is nothing more than a series of stops and starts. Length of view is short and passage along the road becomes a matter of 'follow my leader'. If, however, there are two or three lines of traffic moving in the same direction it is important to be in the correct lane, especially if a turn to left or right is to be made at the next junction.

36 An accurate forecast of traffic movement can sometimes be made by observing quite small details. It is frequently possible to notice something and to link what is seen with the

Figure 9a

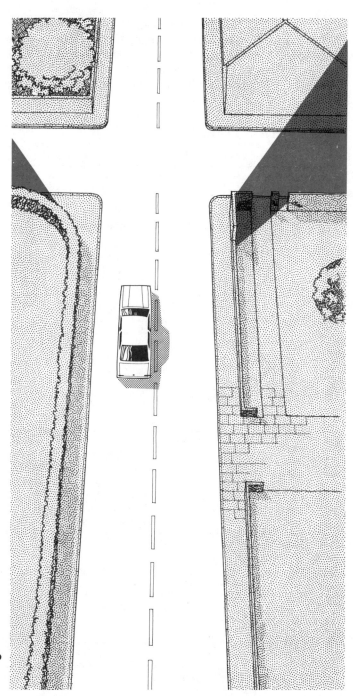

Figure 9b

possibility of something else happening. An obvious example of this is when following a bus. The driver should be aware of the possibility of it stopping farther along the road, particularly if passengers are seen moving towards the exit. A complete list cannot be given but the following further examples will be of use:

OBSERVATION LINKS

Traffic is turning ahead.	Other vehicles may emerge.
Pedestrian hails cab.	Cab may stop suddenly, or turn, or move away from rank. Pedestrian may step into road.
A row of parked vehicles.	Doors may open, vehicles may move off. Pedestrians may step out from between vehicles. Small children may be hidden from view.
Ice cream vans, mobile shops, school buses, etc.	Pedestrians, particularly children, are likely to be in the vicinity.
Bus at stopping place.	Pedestrians crossing road to board or after alighting. Bus moving off possibly at an angle.
Pedal cyclist.	Glancing over shoulder, may then turn right. Strong wind may cause wobble.
Fresh mud or other deposits on road. Newly mown grass, etc.	Slow moving vehicles or animals just around a bend.
Post Office vans, tradesmen's vehicles, etc.	May stop at associated premises, e.g. Post Office, shops, public houses, garages, building sites, etc.
Pull-ins, petrol stations, public houses, parking places, etc.	Movement of vehicles in and out.
Motorway access points.	Vehicles in nearside lane may move out.
Green traffic lights.	May change.

No matter how good a driver's observation may be it can only be of assistance to him if he forms a correct assessment of what he sees and takes the appropriate action or precautions. It is not enough to react merely to what is seen. A positive effort must be made to look for the clues from which an accurate prediction can be made, e.g. shadows on road, reflections in shop windows, exhaust smoke from stationary vehicles, and so on.

Night Driving

37 Whilst this section is headed 'Night Driving' it should be borne in mind that the expression 'Night' in this context applies to the period from the end of the day when light begins to fail until full light the following day. During this time lights must be switched on.

38 In built up areas where visibility is poor dipped headlamps should be used so that the driver's view is extended and other road users can see his vehicle more easily. On unlighted roads the headlamps should be on main beam unless dipped beam is required because of opposing traffic or when following other vehicles. However, there are occasions when dipped headlamps instead of main beam can be used to advantage to illuminate areas which may not otherwise be seen, (e.g. when negotiating left hand bends or at hump back bridges).

39 All lamps must be kept clean and headlamps correctly set so as to provide maximum illumination of the road without causing other drivers to be dazzled. Variation of load can affect beam alignment.

40 One essential fact to be remembered when driving at any time is that the driver should always be in a position to stop his vehicle well within the distance he sees to be clear. Even in ideal conditions, with the windscreen clean inside and out, proper ventilation and correctly aligned headlamps, the driver's view at night is restricted and he should adjust his speed accordingly.

41 A great deal of useful information can be obtained from the front and rear lights of other vehicles. A vehicle ahead approaching a bend from either direction could indicate the severity of the bend by the sweep of the headlights. When following a vehicle its brake lights will provide an early warning of the need to reduce speed. These are only two examples but there are many other occasions when intelligent use of information supplied can be of assistance to the driver.

42 When leaving brightly lit areas speed should be kept down to allow sufficient time for the eyes to become accustomed to the change of environment.

43 Any light inside the vehicle which is allowed to reflect in the windows will cause distraction and affect the driver's ability to see clearly. Most modern vehicles have dials and instruments which are lighted correctly and well cowled; it is mainly interior lights, torches, rally lights and cigarette lighters which will affect vision and the use of these items should be restricted as much as possible.

Dazzle

44 When a driver meets opposing vehicles showing headlights he should refrain from looking directly into them and cast his gaze slightly to the nearside. Should the approaching vehicle have headlights on main beam, a quick flash of the headlamps may serve as a reminder to the other driver. Care should be exercised when doing this to avoid dazzling the other driver and on no account should retaliatory measures be taken. A driver should always be prepared to slow down or stop if he is dazzled, bearing in mind that the eyes need time to re-adjust.

45 When following another vehicle headlamps should be kept in the dipped position and a generous distance between the vehicles allowed so as to prevent the leading driver being dazzled by lights showing in his mirrors. The vehicle should be moved out early prior to overtaking and headlamps kept in the dipped position (except for a quick flash in lieu of a horn warning) until alongside the vehicle being overtaken. In the same way a driver being overtaken should dip his headlights when the following vehicle draws alongside and keep them in that position until they can be raised without dazzling the other driver.

Fatigue

46 Driving at night calls for great concentration and this, combined with dazzle and ever changing conditions of visibility, quickly results in tiredness. Good ventilation and driving with a window open can help to delay the effects but once a driver realises that his driving skills are deteriorating he should reduce speed and, if necessary, stop until he has regained his faculties fully. A walk or a hot drink may be all that is needed but any change from driving will improve the driver's capabilities.

CHAPTER 5

POSITIONING

Introduction
1 The System of Car Control requires at feature 1 that the vehicle be in the correct position at the approach to any hazard. A good driver is always in the correct position on the road, not only when an obvious hazard is present, but at all times. Correct positioning enables the driver to obtain the best possible view of the road ahead and increases his safety margin in relation to the actual and potential danger around him. Positioning is clearly related to many other aspects of driving such as cornering and road observation.

Safety Position
2 This may be defined as the safest position for a vehicle to occupy on a road in relation to the actual and potential dangers existing at that moment.

3 These dangers usually arise from situations on the nearside, such as parked vehicles, pedestrians stepping off the footpath, and concealed junctions. Where such dangers exist it will be safer to take a line nearer the crown of the road to obtain a better view and more space in which to take avoiding action should it become necessary. If because of traffic conditions this plan cannot be adopted, speed must be reduced to ensure that no danger will be caused. Similar safety measures should be taken when driving on the offside of the road in one way systems.

4 When passing a row of stationary vehicles there is always the possibility of a pedestrian stepping out from between them. The view in between these vehicles is always very limited but it can be improved, if traffic conditions permit, by giving them a wide berth and so providing a safety margin as well as a better view.

5 Similarly the view into a road on the nearside can be improved. Figures 10a and b show two cars approaching such a hazard. The driver who is travelling quite close to the nearside cannot see very far into the road on the left and therefore fails to observe the vehicle approaching. The other driver, by positioning well towards the crown of the road, has improved his line of vision and can see the approaching

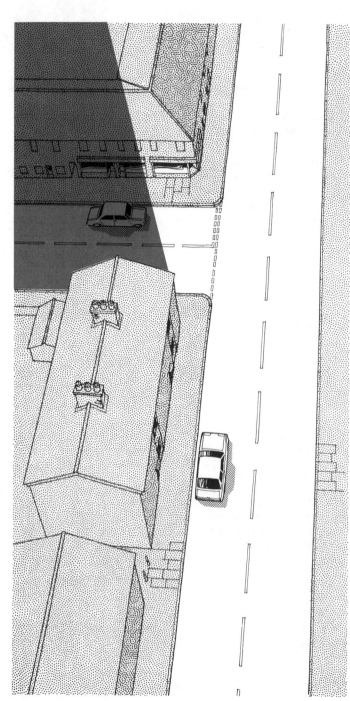

Figure 10a

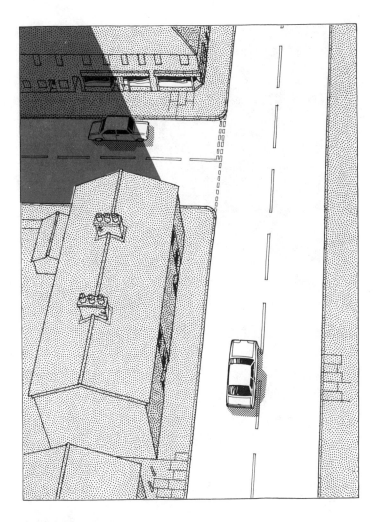

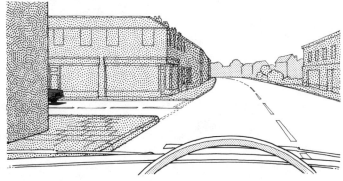

Figure 10b

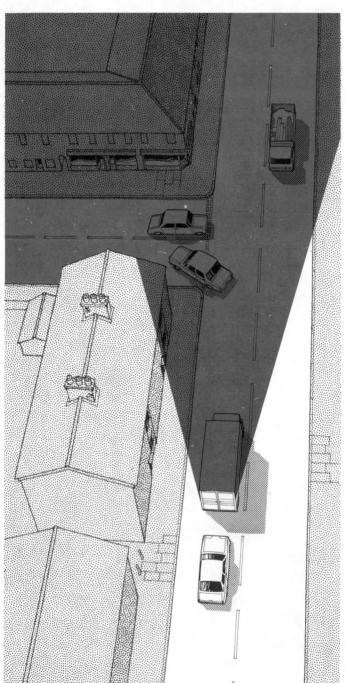

Figure 11a

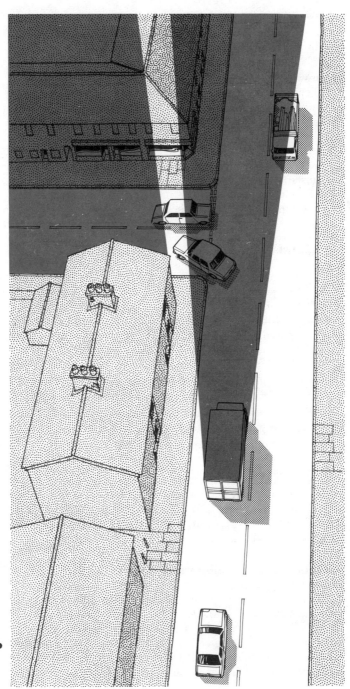

Figure 11b

vehicle. The good driver will always try to ensure not only that he is able to see as much of the road ahead as possible but that other road users can also see him.

Following Position

6 When keeping a position in traffic flows where there is no intention to overtake, a safe distance must be maintained behind the vehicle ahead. As a guide for normal driving conditions one yard per mile per hour should be allowed but in built up areas at speeds below 30 m.p.h. such distances are impracticable if traffic flows are to be maintained. In such circumstances, a minimum distance of one foot per mile per hour should be allowed. (To enable the driver accurately to assess distances, he should bear in mind that an average family car is about 15 feet in length). These distances are the minimum required as stopping distances increase greatly with wet and slippery roads, poor brakes, worn tyres and tired drivers.

7 By keeping at the proper distance from the vehicle in front the driver will gain the following advantages.

(a) He will be able to maintain a good view, which can be increased along the nearside or offside by a very slight deviation, so that he is always aware of what is happening in the immediate vicinity.

(b) He can stop the vehicle safely in the event of the preceding driver braking firmly without warning.

(c) He can extend his braking distance so that a following driver is given more time in which to react.

(d) He can move up into an overtaking position when it is safe to do so.

8 In figure 11a the driver is following too closely to the vehicle in front. He cannot see any of the hazards in the shaded area. In figure 11b he is maintaining a good safety position and all these hazards can then be seen. He can improve his view by moving slightly to his nearside or offside.

Positioning for Turning and Stopping

9 When approaching a junction with the intention of making a left or right turn the driver should position according to the turn, that is to the nearside of the road for a left turn and towards the centre line for a right turn. However, due consideration must be given to traffic light filter arrows, carriageway markings, other traffic and obstructions. Should traffic or road conditions make it necessary, positioning must always be adjusted in the interests of safety. For example, the driver intending to turn right must always be prepared to move away from the centre line when opposing traffic encroaches on his side of the road. Similarly when turning left the acute angle of the corner or the presence of pedestrians may require the approach to be farther out than is normal.

10 When turning right at crossroads, where opposing traffic is carrying out a similar manoeuvre the vehicles should pass off-side to off-side. However, if the road layout makes this difficult or carriageway markings indicate otherwise the vehicles may have to pass nearside to nearside. This will be less safe if the driver's view of approaching vehicles is restricted as he turns.

11 When because of traffic conditions or obstruction of any kind it is necessary for the driver to bring his vehicle to a stand-still he must give thought to his next manoeuvre and position his vehicle so that he can carry out that manoeuvre with the minimum inconvenience to himself or other road users.

12 As a final word on the subject, parking the vehicle must also be considered. It must never be left where it may cause inconvenience or danger to others.

CHAPTER 6

CORNERING

1 Cornering is a term used to describe the driving of a vehicle around a corner or bend. It is an important feature of driving and a thorough understanding of the theory is essential if a safe technique is to be mastered. The manner of approaching and negotiating the various bends and corners encountered in day to day motoring will vary according to the conditions prevailing at each, but the following general principles must be complied with at all times to ensure maximum safety:

Principles
2 (a) Correct positioning of the vehicle on the approach side.

(b) Right choice of speed.

(c) Correct gear for the speed.

(d) The vehicle to maintain constant speed while negotiating the curve.

Safety Factors
3 By application of these principles, the following safety factors will be apparent as the vehicle is about to leave the bend or corner:

(a) It will be on the correct side of the road.

(b) It will be able to remain there.

(c) It will be capable of being stopped in the distance the driver can see to be clear.

Vehicle Roadworthiness
4 The condition of the steering, suspension, shock absorbers, tyres and tyre pressures and the loading of the vehicle will affect the behaviour of the vehicle when negotiating a corner or bend. The driver's responsibility is to ensure that the vehicle and tyres are in good condition, tyre pressures are kept at those recommended by the manufacturer and any load is evenly distributed.

5 The road holding qualities of vehicles vary considerably and an understanding of the characteristics of the vehicle

being driven, together with a sound knowledge of the principles involved, will assist the driver to negotiate a corner or bend with minimum loss of stability.

Cornering Forces

6 A vehicle is most stable when travelling on a straight and level course at a constant speed. When it is driven around a curve certain forces are set up which affect its roadholding capabilities and unless the tyres retain sufficient grip on the road the driver will be unable to maintain his selected course. The forces acting through the centre of gravity of a vehicle are represented in figure 12 by arrows lettered M.C.R.

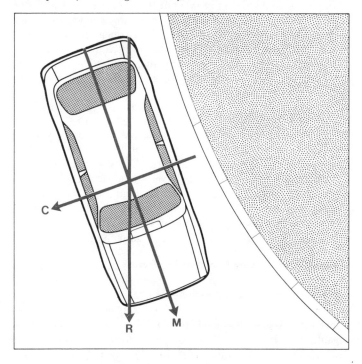

Figure 12

7 Arrow 'M' represents the MOMENTUM of a vehicle which is proportional to its weight and speed. The driver controls the momentum by selecting the correct speed. When the steering wheel is turned to direct the car into a curved path force 'C' is created. This is an outward pull known as CENTRIFUGAL FORCE. In the diagram, which illustrates a curve to the left, a combination of forces M and C produce a 'RESULTANT' force R which tends to take the car towards the offside of the road. Coarse steering or excessive speed may result in a complete loss of stability.

8 Whilst considering the behaviour of a vehicle when cornering it should be stressed that braking at this time is undesirable and may be hazardous. The diagram shows how the weight which is now distributed to the offside wheels on a left hand bend will be thrown forward to the offside front wheel when the brakes are applied. Obviously a vehicle under such stress will be more difficult to handle. In a curve to the right the 'RESULTANT' will be to the nearside.

Road Camber or Cross Fall
9 The camber or cross fall of the road will also have a bearing on the effect of centrifugal force. A normal camber dropping from the crown of the road to kerb will be favourable when negotiating a left hand bend. It would be unfavourable on a right hand bend as the vehicle will tend to slide down the slope more easily. Where the whole width of the road is super elevated with banking, the cross fall will be favourable in either direction, thus reducing the effect of centrifugal force.

The System of Car Control for Bends
10 To apply the principles correctly a driver must be able to appreciate early the different types of bend. This can only be achieved by good advanced observation. It is stressed that merely to observe the road disappearing into a curve will be insufficient. It is essential to look across the bend, for gaps in hedges or between buildings, to look at the road verges, hedgerows and lamp standards, etc., not only to make an assessment of its severity but to seek early warning of additional hazards.

11 Occasions will arise when it is impossible to obtain any information of this nature, leaving only one way to make the assessment. At the approach to most bends the offside and nearside verges appear to meet. This is the limit point of observation. (See figure 13). The rate at which the limit point moves as the vehicle approaches indicates the severity of the

Figure 13

bend, i.e. if on the approach, the limit point appears to remain fixed and the view around the bend does not improve then without doubt the bend is sharp. On the other hand if the limit point begins to move away then a more gradual bend is to be dealt with.

Positioning of the Vehicle on the Approach (Feature One)
12 When approaching any bend the driver must position his vehicle to maintain the best view. From the information thus obtained his position may be adjusted to provide the maximum margin of safety and maintain the maximum stability as he negotiates the bend within the limits of his own half of the road.

Right Hand Bends
13 The correct position on the approach should be close to the nearside. Figures 14a and b show how the view around such a bend is influenced by positioning.

However, before selecting the course consideration must be given to:

(a) Nearside dangers which would require a greater margin of safety, e.g. a blind junction or exit.

(b) Poor condition of road surface on the nearside or adverse camber.

Left Hand Bends
14 On the approach to a left hand bend advantage can often be gained by positioning the vehicle close to the centre line with the object of obtaining an earlier view. Figures 15a and b show how the view around such a bend is influenced by positioning.

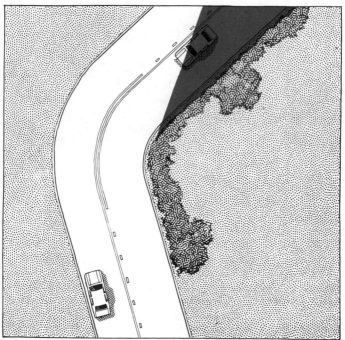

Figure 14a

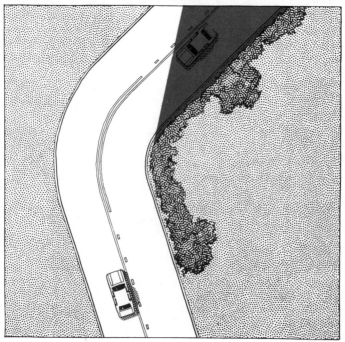

Figure 14b

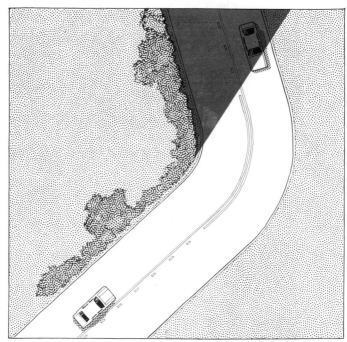

Figure 15a

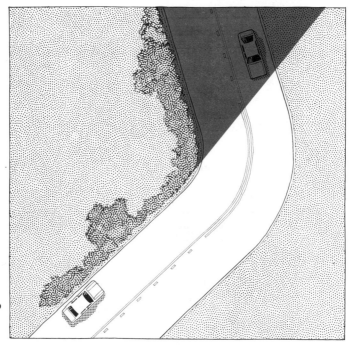

Figure 15b

However, before selecting a course near the centre line, consideration must be given to the following:

(a) Offside dangers which require a greater margin of safety, e.g. approaching traffic.

(b) If such positioning may be misleading to other traffic.

(c) Where no advantage can be gained due to the low speeds involved or the open nature of the bend.

Right Choice of Speed (Feature Two)

15 Mirrors must be used before reducing speed for the bend. Although an arm signal at the approach to a bend is very rarely required it should be considered. Where it is necessary to use the brakes to ensure the correct speed of approach the three rules of braking must be complied with. The right choice of speed will be governed by:

(a) The view into the bend.

(b) The severity of the bend and width of road available.

(c) The state of the road surface.

(d) The actual or possible presence of other road users.

(e) The driver's ability and the road holding qualities of his vehicle.

Correct Gear for the Speed (Feature Three)

16 A safe speed having been achieved the gear must be selected to provide the increased power necessary to drive around the bend at a constant speed with the engine just pulling the vehicle and in which it will respond readily to use of the accelerator.

Mirrors and Signals (Feature Four)

17 A mirror check will ensure that the driver is fully aware of the situation behind before entering the hazard although a signal is not normally required at this point.

Horn (Feature Five)

18 Audible warning of approach is not normally required except perhaps when approaching acute blind bends, particularly on narrow roads where safety margins are restricted.

Acceleration (Feature Six)

19 Ideally the gear selected enables the vehicle to negotiate the bend at a constant speed with the engine just pulling but there will be circumstances where this will not apply and where de-celeration, and even braking may be necessary, for example:

(a) When descending a hill.

(b) Where other traffic makes it unsafe.

20 The point at which acceleration can be applied will be governed by the contours of the road, the state of the road surface and the rate at which a clear view ahead opens up. This point will vary, from just past the apex to where the road straightens.

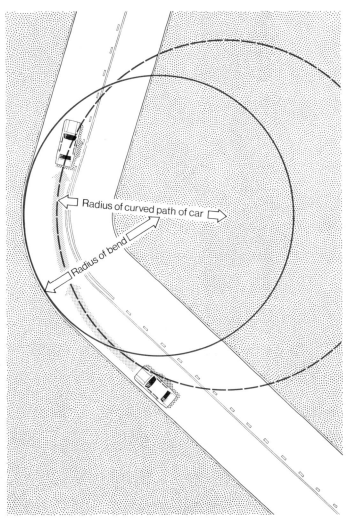

Figure 16

NEGOTIATING THE CURVE

Right Hand Bends

21 Previous paragraphs have dealt with the course selected to obtain the best view when approaching bends. For a right hand bend this was close to the nearside of the road. The driver maintains this course until he can obtain a clear view of the road as it straightens. Having gained this view he selects a gradually curving path towards the centre of the road, provided it is clear. He should then ease the vehicle back towards the nearside of the road. It will be seen from figure 16 that the

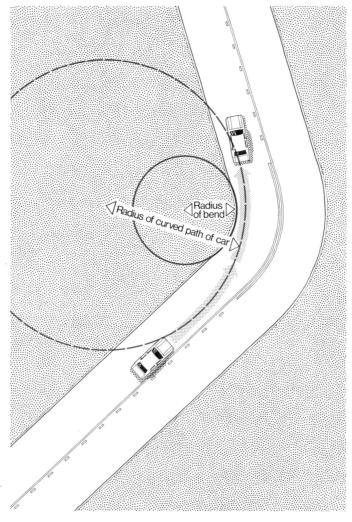

Figure 17

radius of the curved path around the bend exceeds the radius of the bend itself. By following the shallower curve the effect of centrifugal force is reduced thereby improving stability.

Left Hand Bends

22 When negotiating a left hand bend the position towards the centre line is maintained until the view ahead opens up. The vehicle is then driven through a gradual curved path towards the nearside of the road thereby achieving the same advantages as when negotiating a right hand bend (see figure 17).

23 Provided that the driver has positioned correctly and in good time, adjusted speed, chosen the correct gear ratio for the particular type of bend or corner and maintained good observation whilst approaching and negotiating it, there should be no difficulty in achieving the required safety factors. The driver must always position his vehicle according to dangers which become apparent to him. IN NO CIRCUMSTANCES MUST ANY OTHER ROAD USER BE ENDANGERED OR INCONVENIENCED.

CHAPTER 7

OVERTAKING

1 A driver during his journey may pass many stationary and moving vehicles but those travelling in the same direction as himself he is said to 'overtake'. The System of Car Control to be applied to the overtaking manoeuvre is the same as that described for fixed hazards. It is more complex, however, because during the process a number of subsidiary hazards may arise which must be dealt with as the primary hazard itself moves along the road.

2 A stationary vehicle on the nearside of the road requires some thought but presents little difficulty. Frequently the driver need do nothing beyond look in his mirrors before pulling out to pass the obstruction. On other occasions, when approaching traffic makes it unsafe to pass straight away, he must vary his speed and gear; perhaps stop altogether. The horn may need to be sounded if the vehicle is occupied or there are signs of activity in or around it. If the obstruction is not a stationary vehicle but a slowly moving one it is often possible to regard it as stationary for practical overtaking purposes (e.g. a heavy lorry going uphill). As its speed increases planning becomes more difficult and judgment more critical.

3 When a driver realises that he is catching up with another vehicle he makes up his mind either to adjust his speed and follow it while it makes reasonable progress, or overtake at the first opportunity. The decision to overtake is taken soon after the vehicle in front is sighted although the opportunity to do so may not arise for several miles, if at all in some circumstances.

Road Observation
4 Thoughtless overtaking is highly dangerous and observation, planning and attention to detail are of the utmost importance. The overtaking driver must have a full and constant view of the road ahead and an understanding of the possible pitfalls. The course selected at this early stage is the position on the road from which the best view ahead can be gained subject, obviously, to no danger or inconvenience being caused to approaching or following traffic and without encroaching over hazard line markings, etc. Things to be looked for are obstructions on the nearside which may cause the vehicle in

front to move out (possibly without warning), bends, hill crests, junctions, etc., where overtaking is dangerous and, on roads carrying two-way traffic, approaching vehicles. Painted lines on roads give warning of approach to hazards and arrows give an indication of a double line system ahead.

Planning

5 At most places where overtaking is forbidden by the Highway Code the dangers are self-evident but many drivers overtake quite happily at junctions in the belief that traffic emerging from a side road will allow them right of way. Figures 18-22 illustrate some common accident situations when overtaking at junctions.

6 When overtaking the driver should aim to comply with the following:

(a) Never cause the overtaken or an approaching vehicle to alter course or speed;

(b) Avoid making a third line of vehicles abreast, either travelling in the same or opposite directions;

(c) Always be able to move back into the nearside in plenty of time.

7 In the absence of approaching vehicles or other hazard the driver need only check the mirrors, move out on to a course to pass the vehicle with plenty of room and move back to the nearside of the road after overtaking without cutting in. No change in speed or gear may be necessary from when the vehicle is first seen to when it is overtaken and the only other feature of the System to be actually applied may be the horn. However, more often than not an approaching vehicle, bend, hill crest, etc., will be seen and a decision taken as to whether the overtake can be completed safely before arrival at the hazard or not. On the approach to a bend or hill crest this means making allowances for a fast vehicle coming into view from the opposite direction. Judgments must be made in which experience plays a great part and must include an assessment of the speed of vehicles concerned and distances involved, such as:

(a) Speed of vehicles to be overtaken.

(b) Speed and performance of own vehicle.

(c) Speed of approaching vehicle(s) in view.

Figure 18
Driver 'B' moves out looking to his right as 'A' approaches on wrong side of road.

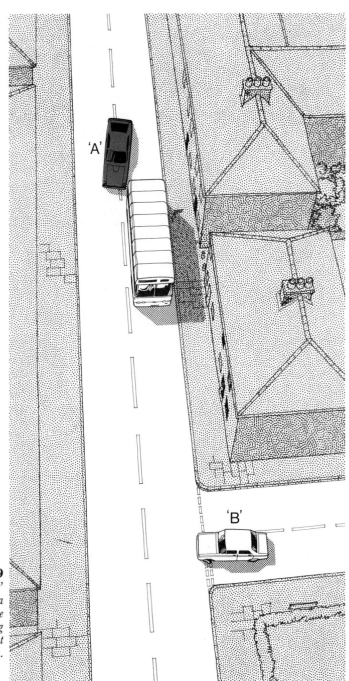

Figure 19
*Driver 'B'
sees only a
slow vehicle
approaching
and moves out
as 'A' overtakes.*

(d) Possible high speed of approaching vehicles as yet unseen.

(e) Distance available to overtake and re-gain nearside relative to (a) to (d) above.

The safe maxim is 'IF IN DOUBT HOLD BACK'.

8 Road observation will vary from immediate foreground through middle distance to far distance and back again with frequent glances in the mirror. It is not enough just to see everything, the correct interpretation has to be made. The driver of a small, crowded saloon car in front may have his attention diverted between what is going on inside and outside the car. A delivery van driver approaching a parade of shops may see his delivery point at the last moment and swerve suddenly across the road. Similarly, the long distance driver may turn off into a cafe. A high vehicle or caravan could be affected by a side wind. The type of vehicle to be overtaken must therefore be taken into account, as must the performance of the vehicle being driven. For instance if driving a low powered car and wishing to overtake a heavily laden lorry, the best time maybe when going uphill as the speed of the lorry falls.

9 Different types of road present different problems, which will vary according to

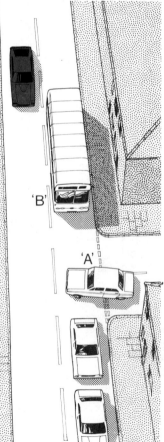

Figure 20
Driver 'A' is beckoned out by driver 'B' into path of overtaking car.

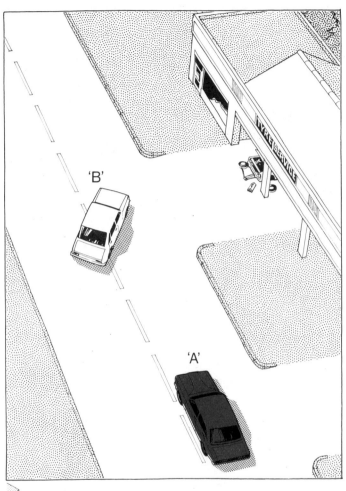

Figure 21
*Vehicle 'B'
turns without
warning into
an entrance as
'A' goes to
overtake.*

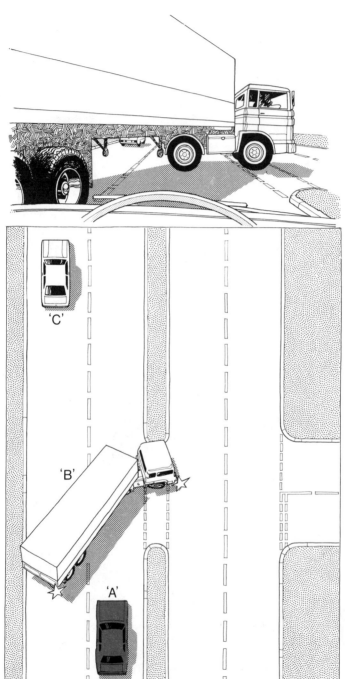

Figure 22
Driver 'A' fails to appreciate that driver 'B' is not overtaking vehicle 'C'.

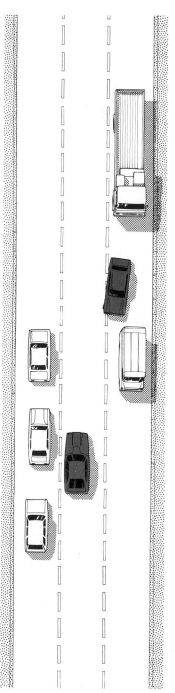

Figure 23

whether they are in the country or in town, but the condition of the road surface is always a factor to be taken into account. There may be ruts which can throw a vehicle off line or surface water which will result in a curtain of spray at a critical moment.

10 The most dangerous road carrying two way traffic is the one marked with three lanes, the overtaking lane each way being the centre lane. Overtaking must not be attempted on such a road if there is the possibility of an approaching vehicle moving out into the centre lane or when the overtaking vehicle would make a third line of moving vehicles, 'The meat in the sandwich'. (See figure 23).

11 When judging speed and distance to overtake with a vehicle approaching, the "lurker" must be looked for, i.e. the small fast car or motor cycle which closes right up behind a lorry and then swoops out into full view. (See figure 24).

12 It cannot be assumed that the driver of a light vehicle or car following a heavy lorry is content to remain where he is. He has probably been following too closely and with no idea of what lies ahead. He could pull out to take a look just as a following driver accelerates to overtake both vehicles.

Figure 24

13 The temptation to follow another vehicle through an apparently safe gap must be resisted. The leading vehicle could slip into a place of safety in the nearside leaving the trusting follower stranded in the middle lane faced by oncoming traffic. (See figure 25).

14 Each driver must make up his own mind when it is safe to overtake and, when passing several slower moving vehicles, always have a gap in the nearside lane into which he can pull if necessary without cutting in. (See figure 26).

15 Dual carriageways eliminate the need to assess the speed and distance of approaching vehicles but otherwise still demand the same degree of care. Speeds are mainly higher and drivers tend to move out from the nearside to change lane with less regard for following traffic. The wider the road the more this occurs, especially on motorways. As the overtaking position is approached vehicles in the nearside, and the middle lane if appropriate, must be watched. If one of them is closing up on a vehicle in front it is certainly going to pull out, possibly with no signal but probably with a trafficator switched on at the same time as the steering wheel is turned. A good guide is to note the distance between the wheels of a vehicle and the lane markings. If the gap narrows it could be moving out. Overtaking at a time which would cause three vehicles to be abreast of each other should be avoided, if possible.

16 It is often possible by the use of acceleration sense to vary the speed a little on the approach so as to arrive at the overtaking position just at the right time. Where this is not possible speed will be reduced to that of the leading vehicle in order to follow in line at a safe distance.

17 From his 'Safety Position' (See Chapter 5) the driver having decided that an overtaking opportunity is developing may move up into an overtaking position. The view ahead must be maintained for movement of other traffic, parked vehicles and other obstructions and any physical feature of the road which may make it unsafe to overtake.

Right Hand Bend

18 Where the leading vehicle is approaching a bend to the right where the view is restricted the following driver should select a course well to the nearside, moving up on the vehicle in front just before it reaches the apex of the bend so that he gains the earliest possible view along its offside (See figure 27). If conditions are favourable a straight course should be adopted to overtake with adequate

Figure 25

nearside clearance. If conditions are not favourable for overtaking the driver must drop back and resume his safety position.

Left Hand Bend

19 Where the leading vehicle is approaching a blind bend to the left the following driver must not attempt to overtake until the road is straight. He should maintain a position where he can see along the nearside of the leading vehicle as it passes through the bend. If this view is favourable he may move out to look along the offside as the road straightens and start to overtake when conditions are suitable (See figure 28), bearing in mind that when changing from a nearside to an offside view, areas of the road ahead will be obscured. Great care must be taken when carrying out this manoeuvre.

System of Car Control

20 When conditions are suitable to overtake the course is selected to pass with plenty of room bearing in mind that the higher the speed the greater the margin required for safety. A glance in the mirrors will be necessary to see if a signal need be given before moving out (System of Car Control, Feature One). If already on course to pass, no signal will be given. At Feature Two the mirrors will be checked again but a signal would not be needed nor would speed be adjusted. At Feature

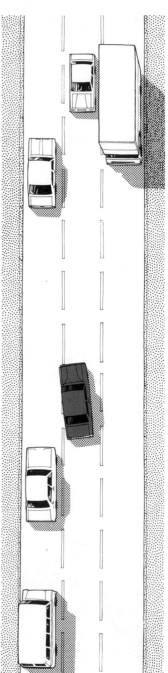

Figure 26

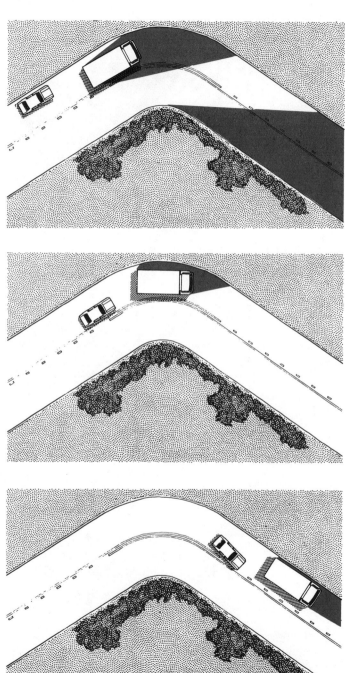

Figure 27

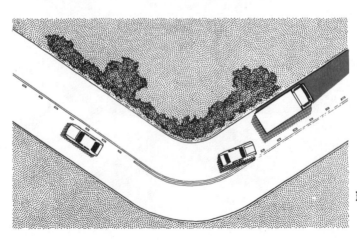

Figure 28

Three the gear will be considered to give the best acceleration within the speed ranges to be used in the manoeuvre, although the alert driver should already be in the right gear. A final glance in the mirrors at Feature Four is worthwhile but no signal would normally be of any use at this point. The horn (Feature Five) is frequently a vital safety factor, particularly if more than one vehicle is to be passed at once or there is a possibility that the driver in front may not be aware of the presence of the overtaking vehicle.

21 A vehicle travelling alongside another vehicle is in a zone of danger in which it does not do to dwell too long. Overtaking should therefore be completed as quickly as possible (Feature Six) but before he reaches the rear of the vehicle in front the driver still has an opportunity to change his mind and drop back.

22 Overtaking calls for judgment and expertise which can be acquired only by experience and practice. As skill and the judgment of speed and distance are developed mistakes may be made. It is important for the driver to realise this and for him to make sure that his decisions err on the side of safety. Patience must be exercised at all times and a margin of safety left for error.

CHAPTER 8

SKIDDING

1 Skidding is defined as:
    The involuntary movement of the vehicle due to the grip of the tyres on the road becoming less than a force or forces acting on the vehicle. In other words a vehicle skids when one or more of the tyres lose normal grip on the road.

2 Any driver who has experienced a skid will remember that he was changing either the speed or direction of the vehicle immediately prior to the skid developing. It will therefore be realised that skids are usually caused by accelerating, braking or changing direction, these manoeuvres being carried out so suddenly or forcibly that forces are created which are more powerful than the grip of the tyres on the road. It therefore follows that the more slippery the road surface the less powerful these forces need be to break the grip of the tyres.

3 Figure 29 shows a plan of a car and the forces which may operate are indicated by arrows:

(a) Is created by acceleration.

(b) Is created by de-celeration (usually by braking).

(c) Sideways forces created by the driver who steers the vehicle to the left or right.

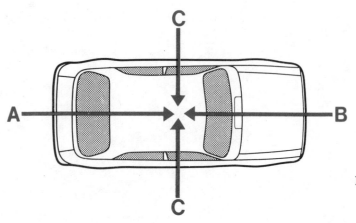

Figure 29

These forces act on a vehicle when a driver operates the controls, but they should never be permitted to become so powerful as to overcome the grip of the tyres on the road. Two of these forces are combined when the vehicle follows a curved path when under the influence of braking or acceleration.

4 The following are the causes of skidding, either singly or in combination:

(a) Excessive speed for the existing circumstances—this is a basic cause.

(b) Coarse steering in relation to a speed which is not in itself excessive.

(c) Harsh acceleration.

(d) Excessive or sudden braking.

Recognition and Correction of Skids
5 It is essential that each type of skid is recognised in the early stages of development if corrective measures are to be taken.

Rear Wheel Skid
6 This occurs when the rear wheels lose their grip on the road and the vehicle may swing in either direction. It can be caused by (a) (b) (c) or (d) of paragraph 4 and if unchecked can cause the vehicle to turn broadside or completely around.

Eliminate the cause by relaxing pressure on the accelerator or brake pedal and at the same time turn the steering wheel in the direction of the skid, i.e. if the rear wheels slide to the left, turn the steering wheel to the left. When stability has been regained the vehicle can be steered on to the desired course. Excess or prolonged steering correction should be avoided or another skid may be induced in the opposite direction.

Front Wheel Skid
7 This occurs usually on a corner or bend when the front wheels lose their grip and the vehicle does not travel in the direction in which it is being steered. It can be caused by (a) (b) and (d) of paragraph 4 and in the case of a front wheel drive vehicle also by (c) of that paragraph. Eliminate the cause by relaxing the accelerator or brakes, momentarily straighten the steering to allow the front wheels to regain their grip and then gently steer on to course. In a front wheel drive vehicle the driver should be prepared for the sudden grip of the front wheels as de-celeration becomes effective.

Four Wheel Skid

8 This occurs when all wheels lose their grip on the road. It is usually associated with (d) of paragraph 4 and the effect on the vehicle may be a combination of those encountered in a rear or front wheel skid. On slippery surfaces the driver may experience a sensation of an increase rather than a decrease of speed.

The next action will normally be dictated by traffic conditions but usually there is need for a quick reduction in speed. On dry roads this will be achieved by maintaining the pressure on the brake pedal. Where, however, directional control is more important, and in all cases on wet or slippery roads, the cause of the skid must be eliminated by relaxing the pressure on the brake pedal, thus allowing the wheels to again revolve to regain control. On wet or slippery roads maximum de-celeration may be gained by cadence braking. (See Chapter 2 paragraph 33). It should be remembered that a four wheel skid may also be a progression from a front or rear wheel skid which has not been corrected.

To Minimise the Risk of Skidding

9 Every driver should aim to drive and control the vehicle in such a way that it does not skid. However this becomes increasingly difficult as road and weather conditions deteriorate. Good road observation with accurate interpretation of what is seen is necessary in order that road conditions may be accurately evaluated and speed adjusted accordingly.

10 Some obvious hazards such as snow and ice are recognised by most drivers as dangerous surfaces. Few appreciate that a shower of rain after a long dry period can produce conditions where skidding may occur because the accumulation of rubber-dust and oil together with water creates a very slippery surface.

11 Almost every type of surface gives a reasonable grip to the tyres at very low speeds but as speed increases this grip value falls rapidly on some surfaces and recognition of potentially dangerous areas is essential. Some examples are given in Chapter 4 paragraphs 18 to 25. To realise the surface is bad only when the vehicle is running over it is too late.

12 The importance of an adequate depth of tread and correct pressure in the tyres must again be stressed as neglect of these factors will increase the risk on slippery roads.

13 When driving on very slippery roads smooth control is essential. Any braking, steering or gear changing must be carried out so that tyre adhesion is not broken. When moving off or travelling at low speeds the selection of a higher gear than normal may be advantageous to reduce the possibility of wheel spin.

General

14 If a skid is allowed to develop fully a driver will rarely find that he has enough space to correct it. Concentration and good observation are essential if skids are to be avoided and quick reactions are necessary when a skid does occur.

It is important again to stress that on very slippery roads the best control of speed is through the accelerator with a suitable gear engaged.

Reduction of the speed on a slippery surface is best done by the selection of a lower gear but it is essential that the gear change is made as smoothly as possible with accurate matching of engine revolutions to the road speed before the clutch is finally engaged.

15 Skidding instruction is given for three reasons:

(a) To raise the standard of driving, to give the highest degree of all round efficiency;

(b) To give confidence in driving under any conditions; and,

(c) To equip the driver to meet any emergency which might arise.

SKIDDING MUST NOT BE PRACTISED ON PUBLIC ROADS.

CHAPTER 9

SPEED AND SAFETY

General

1 Improvements in vehicle design and road engineering over the years have led to vehicles capable of achieving and maintaining a high speed with safety, especially on roads designed for this purpose. Without a similar raising of driving standards any advantages offered by such improvements will be lost. Not every driver is capable or desirous of using these improvements to maintain high speeds and, of course, not every road is suitable. Speed is frequently looked upon as something dangerous in itself, but it is dangerous only if used in the wrong place or at the wrong time. Speed then is a relative thing.

2 What to a novice may be a dangerous speed is not necessarily so to a more experienced driver. The choice of speed must be related to the driver's ability, the type, condition and limitations of the vehicle and the prevailing road and traffic conditions, bearing in mind that the safe speed for any given section of road may vary from minute to minute as circumstances alter.

3 Statutory speed restrictions in respect of areas and classes of vehicles assist in reducing instances of dangerous high speed but legislation by itself is not sufficient for on many occasions the maximum permitted speed will be too fast for safety. Remember the onus is always on the driver to select a speed appropriate to the conditions, for example, although 30 m.p.h. may be permitted through a shopping area to drive at that speed at certain times of the day might be positively dangerous.

Speed—its Affects on the Driver

4 How vision is affected by speed has been mentioned previously, but the importance of first class observation again needs to be stressed. Observation is seeing and assessing the road ahead to enable a safe driving plan to be made. This becomes more difficult as speeds increase. Travelling slowly a driver can afford to direct his attention to things in the immediate foreground. Although a driver should automatically focus his eyes and attention farther ahead when driving faster, few fully appreciate the importance of making a special effort to do this by varying the length and width of vision to take in the most distant features and not miss important lateral detail.

5 After travelling at fairly fast speeds upon the open roads, it will be noticed that when speed is brought down to 30 m.p.h. on entering a restricted area it seems as if the vehicle is crawling along. After a while the sensation of travelling slower than the limit disappears but it will always recur following an appreciable reduction in speed after driving fast for a prolonged period on the open road. In these circumstances it is always advisable to look at the speedometer before entering a restricted area, roundabout or other hazard. Be especially careful when leaving a motorway.

6 A frequent check on the speedometer is always valuable as speed is difficult to judge in some circumstances. When travelling along narrow and winding country lanes even moderate speeds appear to be high while the impression of travelling fast would not be apparent on an open road at that speed. At night, or in conditions of reduced visibility, speed is deceptive and may be much higher than the driver realises. The driver of a quality car should not be misled into thinking that the speed of the vehicle is lower than it is in reality due to the lack of noise and vibration which may be present in less expensive production cars.

7 Travelling at high speed requires total concentration and mental application. If these speeds are maintained over considerable distances fatigue will result. The driver should also be aware of the danger of being called upon to drive at a high speed after prolonged periods of driving at normal speeds. He may already be tired or not mentally attuned to the task and must make allowances or errors of judgment will result.

Use of Speed

8 Efficiency in driving at speed is not easily acquired. Every driver has his own speed limit, the highest speed at which he is perfectly safe and comfortable in any given situation. He should never attempt to go beyond that limit for if he does he may be late to react to an emergency. When circumstances make it necessary to drive at high speed it is of vital importance to remember and put into practice all that is set out in this manual. At 30 m.p.h. a minor driving error can be rectified. At 70 m.p.h. the same error can have disastrous consequences.

9 Speed must be governed at all times by the amount of road that can be seen to be clear, therefore high speeds are safe only when a clear view of the road ahead is possible for a considerable distance. A driver must always be able to stop within the range of his vision by day or by night. In this respect local knowledge can be a dangerous thing as it is tempting to drive faster than is safe on a familiar road. Many people drive too fast where hazards exist because they do not recognise actual or potential danger and in the belief that they will be able to stop whatever happens. A driver should not only know his stopping distances but be able to relate them to the road on which he is travelling. On a single track road due allowance must be made at all times for the possibility that another vehicle may appear around the next bend. Because of the combined speeds the distance available for braking may be halved.

As may be seen from the table in Chapter 2, if speed is doubled then the braking distance is quadrupled, i.e. speed 30 m.p.h.—braking distance 45 feet. Speed 60 m.p.h.—braking distance 180 feet.

10 When driving fast the need to overtake other vehicles will occur more frequently. Overtaking is a potentially dangerous manoeuvre and must be carried out as quickly as possible. It will always call for accurate judgment of the distances involved and the speed of any approaching vehicle. The speed of the vehicle to be overtaken must also be considered but generally this is easier to determine because it can be judged by the speed at which it is being overhauled.

11 Adverse weather conditions no matter what the cause, be it rain, snow, fog or wind, may demand a drastic reduction in speed to keep within the bounds of safety. If the road surface is wet then the allowance for braking distance should be at least doubled whilst on icy stretches it could be in excess of four times that required in normal circumstances.

12 High speeds on stretches of road affected by heavy rain or surface water can be hazardous and lead to 'Aqua Planing'. This is a condition in which the front tyres lose contact with the road surface due to the formation of a wedge of water which forces itself between tyre and road. This results in loss of steering control. If a driver suspects that his vehicle is or is about to aqua plane the application of brakes even momentarily may aggravate the condition by breaking the last small contact between tyre and road. Control will not be regained until speed has been reduced by deceleration.

Under normal motoring conditions the factors necessary for true aqua planing are heavy rain, a smooth tyre, a smooth or badly drained road and a speed in excess of 50 m.p.h.

Extremes of any of these conditions permit the others to be less stringent.

13 A driver should always take time to familiarise himself with the controls and characteristics of a vehicle to which he is unaccustomed before attempting to drive fast.

To Sum Up:

(a) Do not drive at high speeds unless you are competent and it is safe to do so.

(b) Do not relax for an instant. Use all your skill and concentration.

(c) Always drive so that you can pull up in the range of your vision whether by day or by night.

(d) If you double your speed you quadruple your braking distance.

(e) Put into practice all principles covered in other chapters.

(f) Guard against the effects of fatigue.

(g) No emergency is so urgent as to justify an accident. It is far better to arrive late than not at all.

CHAPTER 10

GENERAL ADVICE AND TEN COMMANDMENTS

Condition of Vehicle
1 Every driver is responsible for ensuring that his vehicle is in a roadworthy condition and the following items should be checked:

(a) Visual examination of exterior for damage or defects.

(b) Hand brake on and gear lever in neutral.

(c) Tools.

(d) Wheels—make sure they are secure.

(e) Tyres—check the pressure, tread depth and damage including spare. (Tyre pressure readings will not be accurate unless the tyre is cold).

(f) Oil, water, windscreen washer bottle and other fluid levels as necessary.

(g) Fan belt—for wear and tension.

(h) Lights—including indicators and stop lights.

(i) Windscreen wipers/washers.

(j) Horn.

(k) Fire extinguisher.

(l) Seat belts—ensure they run freely and are not frayed, etc.

Pre Driving Check
2 Before moving off the driver should familiarise himself with the position and operation of the controls and instruments. The following routine should be carried out:

(a) Ensure the hand brake is on and check both hand and foot brake operation.

(b) Check that the gear lever is in neutral.

(c) Adjust seat, mirrors and steering wheel as appropriate.

(d) Check doors for security.

(e) Check position of controls and auxiliaries.

(f) Switch on ignition; note warning lights, start engine. (Choke to be used as required in accordance with manufacturer's directions). Check instrument readings and warning lights. Ensure sufficient fuel for journey.

All seat belts to be worn and properly adjusted. As soon as possible after moving off the driver should carry out a running brake test (see Chapter 2 paragraph 34) and at the same time check the operation of the seat belts. At intervals throughout the journey all instruments and warning lights should be checked and necessary action taken if a fault is indicated.

Stopping and Leaving Vehicle

3 When intending to leave the vehicle the driver should bring it to rest in the most convenient and safe position, close to the kerb if on a road. The foot should remain on the brake pedal until the hand brake is applied and neutral is selected. The engine and unwanted auxiliaries should then be switched off and the seat belt neatly secured. An automatic gearbox should be left in P position and with a manual gearbox it may be desirable to select either first or reverse gear when parking on a gradient. The driver should look in his mirrors and over his shoulder before he or other occupants open a door. The vehicle should be properly secured if it is to be left unattended.

Hints on Reversing

4 One of the most difficult manoeuvres is that of reversing, particularly in confined areas. When driving forward the vehicle is seen to respond to the action of the steering but in reversing the steering effect is delayed and is different in response and feel. (See also Chapter 2 paras 44-45). The higher the speed the more difficult it is to steer accurately. It is, therefore, essential that any reversing is carried out at a slow speed with delicate use of the clutch, accelerator and brake pedals. It must be borne in mind that the brakes may be less effective when the vehicle is in reverse.

Before reversing the driver should:
  (a) Scan the area for obstructions and suitability.

  (b) Ensure that all windows are clear and an unobstructed view is available.

  (c) Obtain assistance if available.

When reversing:
  (a) Travel slowly, slipping the clutch as necessary. In

automatics the speed may be checked by use of the left foot on the brake.

(b) Remember that as the steering is turned the front of the vehicle moves out and may strike nearby objects.

(c) Be prepared to turn the head in any direction to ensure every area of potential danger is observed.

(d) In poor visibility in the absence of reversing lights illuminate the area to the rear of the vehicle by using the brake lights or directional indicators taking care not not to mislead other road users.

Driving through Water

5 To drive at speed into water may wrench the front wheels out of line and cause the driver to lose control. Particular care is necessary at night when the difference between a wet road surface and flood water is difficult to detect. Flood water will collect quickly at the sides of a cambered road, where the road is undulating, where there is a dip under a bridge and in poorly drained low lying areas.

On the approach to flooded areas reduce speed considerably and avoid driving through water if possible by making intelligent use of the unaffected parts of the road. If, however, this is not possible choose the shallowest section to drive through, bearing in mind that there may be hidden obstructions or subsidence. If the route is entirely submerged stop the vehicle and assess the situation. The depth of water which can be successfully negotiated varies with the type of vehicle having regard to the height of the body and the position of the electrical components. Having decided to drive on, the following procedure should be adopted:

(a) Engage first gear and keep the engine running fast by slipping the clutch. On automatics apply sufficient pressure to the foot brake to prevent the vehicle from gaining speed whilst maintaining the necessary engine revolutions. In this way the water will be prevented from entering the exhaust pipe.

(b) Maintain a slow and even speed to avoid making a bow wave.

(c) Immediately after passing through deep water drive slowly with the brakes lightly applied with the left foot until they grip. Repeat the operation after a short time until satisfied that brake efficiency has been fully restored.

Broken Windscreen

6 A frequent cause is a stone thrown up from the wheels of another vehicle or shaken from a gravel lorry. Precautions should be taken on roads where loose stones or grit are present by reducing speed and if following another vehicle holding back farther than normal.

This is an emergency. Generally it is not advisable to punch a hole in the screen to gain vision as this may aggravate the situation by allowing pieces of glass to enter the car and cause injuries. All that is necessary is to pull into the side of the road as soon as possible and stop.

If it is necessary to continue to drive the screen should be pushed outwards and as much glass removed as possible. The body work and air vents should be protected. The vehicle should be driven slowly to protect the driver and passengers against glass splinters. If suitable spectacles are available they should be worn.

TEN COMMANDMENTS OF MOTORING

1 Perfect your Roadcraft

Roadcraft includes every aspect of driving and can be acquired only by a systematic approach to hazards and constant application of the basic rules. Good roadcraft enables a driver to avoid awkward and possibly dangerous situations. It not only prevents accidents but makes driving less arduous.

— *Use your skill to keep out of trouble.*

2 Drive with deliberation and overtake as quickly as possible

Good driving demands continual planning and correct decisions which must be put into operation with deliberation. There is no place for the half-hearted manoeuvre born of doubt or uncertainty. If it is not completely safe it should not be attempted at all.

Overtaking should always be completed in the minimum of time to leave the road clear for approaching or following vehicles.

— *Deliberation eliminates uncertainty. When safe, go!*

3 Develop car sense and know the capabilities of your vehicle

Car sense is the ability to get the best from the vehicle without jerks or vibration. Before a strange vehicle is driven fast the driver should accustom himself to its controls, acceleration and braking capabilities and handling characteristics. Never expect more from them than they are able to give. Vehicles, like drivers, have their limitations.

—*Driver and vehicle must blend to ensure skilful driving.*

4 Give proper signals, use the horn and headlights thoughtfully

Use the signals given in the Highway Code. An ambiguous signal is misleading and dangerous. Use of the horn is a form of signalling much neglected by some and overdone by others. It should be used as a person would use his voice, neither aggressively nor rudely. Flashing the lights is an efficient form of signalling at night and on fast roads.

—*Give good signals in good time.*

5 Concentrate all the time to avoid accidents

Concentration is the keystone of good driving. It is a primary duty but often a neglected one. Complete concentration will ensure that every detail is observed. It is often the smallest detail that gives the clue to what is about to happen. If it is missed an accident, or at least an unpleasant experience, may result.

—*Concentration assists observation.*

6 Think before acting

The good driver makes progress so smoothly and with so little apparent fuss or effort that to the uninitiated he appears to respond to situations automatically. Nothing could be farther from the truth. The fact is that by continuous concentration and thought he has raised his driving to a fine art.

Every hazard and driving operation presents problems which can only be solved by thinking. A thoughtful driver applies the appropriate features of the System, carries out every operation and manoeuvre in plenty of time and consequently is always in the right place at the right moment.

— *Think and avoid accidents.*

7 Exercise restraint and hold back when necessary

To hold back is to follow a vehicle at a safe distance until road and traffic conditions allow it to be overtaken. This will call for restraint especially when in a hurry. Overtaking or any other manoeuvre must never be attempted unless it can be completed with 100 per cent safety. Accidents are caused because a situation has been wrongly assessed.

— *Whenever in doubt, wait.*

8 Corner with safety

Driving around a curve demands the application of the principles for cornering and a thorough knowledge of the forces acting on the vehicle. The most common faults are entering too fast or accelerating before the exit is clearly seen.

> *—Lose your speed or lose the car.*

9 Use speed intelligently and drive fast only in the right places

High speeds are safe only when a clear view is available for a considerable distance and there is time to assess each hazard as it appears, but speed at all times must be related to the view. Safety with speed depends largely upon ability to recognise danger and to slow down in good time.

> *—Any fool can drive fast enough to be dangerous.*

10 Know the Highway Code and put it into practice

The Highway Code sets out rules for safety on the road. A failure to observe them could establish liability in any legal proceedings. The rules must be known and complied with if a driver's own behaviour is to be beyond reproach and before he can presume to advise others. The Highway Code urges all to be courteous. A good driver goes farther and acknowledges the courtesies extended to him.

> *—Drive according to the Highway Code and you will drive safely.*

Printed in the United Kingdom for HMSO
Dd292641 3/90 C440 G3390 10170

NOTES